NICE RENDITION

Cheryl Wheeler's Lyrics In Calligraphy

To JJ + Jerra —

Cheryl Wheeler

This book is **0719** of 2000.

MARSH MICHAELS

All lyrics written by Cheryl Wheeler
© Penrod and Higgins Music - ACF Music Group
PO Box 1770 Hendersonville TN 37077

MARSH
MICHAELS

196 Lasell Street · Boston, MA 02132
marshmichaels@verizon.net · 617-835-6565

www.nicerendition.com

Photography by Aimee Michaels
Proofreading by Carole Marsh, Cheryl Wheeler, Mr. Magoo
Layout and Design by Aimee Michaels
Created in CS3 on an iMac
Typefaces used: Optima, Adobe Garamond Pro Semi Bold
Nice Rendition title lettering by Mary Lawler
Dust jacket design by Mary Lawler

ISBN: 978-0-9827523-0-2

This book was produced with zero VOC inks on SFC Certified paper,
boards and cloth materials, using renewable electricity by:
Dynagraf, Canton, MA an EPA Green Energy Certified Partner

TABLE OF CONTENTS

FORWARD

Astonished. When Aimee Michaels and Carole Marsh **asked my permission** to make this book I was astonished. Permission? Were they kidding? What songwriter wouldn't want this? Apparently I've won some sort of cosmic lottery, without even buying a ticket. Well.... thank you, all of you wonderful artists, for your extraordinary and beautiful work. I am at a loss for, of all things, words, to express my appreciation and gratitude.

I have loved everything about the alphabet ever since I've known there was one. Letters are just so beautiful, I loved learning upper and lower case Printing and Cursive. B was always my favorite. And then, look what they do! Just 26 symbols, communicating.... everything. It seems impossible. I wear a ring with the alphabet on it. It's the only piece of jewelry I wear. To me, it's a sort of devotion, like I'm going steady with the alphabet. Yes, and loving every minute.

Cheryl Wheeler

They march in any order
they change the way they speak
they notify the president
and lull the babe to sleep
all hail these brilliant twenty six
with naught but curves
and balls and sticks
they've handled every word I've said
every book I've ever read
every missive, every note
every song I ever wrote

by Cheryl Wheeler
Calligraphy by Dan Mooney

INTRODUCTION

Nice Rendition: Cheryl Wheeler's Lyrics in Calligraphy was created with love and friendship. Feeling the post-concert magic of a Cheryl Wheeler show and seeing Aimee's starry eyes as she talked of the upcoming International Calligraphy Conference in Boston, sparked the idea for this book in Carole. Aimee, filled with love of Cheryl's songs, lettering, and the calligraphic community, assembled this talented and generous group of calligraphers who made our vision a reality. We are very proud to present their inspiring artwork which combines Cheryl's striking lyrics with the beauty of calligraphy.

Cheryl Wheeler is a prolific songwriter. This collection of her songs is a sampling of the range of her material. Some of these songs have been recorded, some have not. Some were written long ago, some more recently. We highly recommend seeking out all her music.

This book of Cheryl's lyrics attempts to answer the question: what if we could only see the songs? The lettering style, color palette, and mark of the tool translate the overall emotional content of the song. The speed of the strokes on the page are determined by the time signature and tempo. They are punctuated by whole, half, quarter, sixteenth and dotted notes of intensity. Major chords of bright and cheerful colors are juxtaposed against minor chords of darker hues. Each letter is a note of color. Each phrase is a chord of pleasing tones. Each song is a complete picture.

Art is both transformative and healing. Cheryl put her pen to paper and wrote these lyrics. We have been forever changed by her songs. They have been included in our most joyful celebrations and offered us comfort during our most despairing moments. This book is a celebration of Cheryl's words as well as the art of calligraphy.

So please join us. Put on your comfy clothes. Sit in that favorite chair, maybe with a furry companion by your side. Take hold of this book. You are now an important part of this amazing journey. Enjoy.

Carole Marsh and Aimee Michaels

DRIVING HOME

I was drivin' home
By the river side
Richard Thompson on
And the day so fine
Pennsylvania towns
Sort of slip right by
In a soft line south
Under purple skies

I was drivin' home
Through the Sunday bells
Through the trailer towns
Through the rolling hills
From behind some cloud
The sun still shines
And the streams run down
The mountain sides

Slow down what's the hurry
There's no rush today
There won't be too many
Days like today

I was drivin' home
On the black top tar
Up and down this road
Like a cartoon car
Mason-Dixon line
Slips behind me now
Golden fields go by
Golden sun goes down

Slow down what's the hurry
There's no rush today
There won't be too many
Days like today

Driving home ...
Driving home ...

I WAS DRIVIN' HOME
BY THE RIVER SIDE
RICHARD THOMPSON ON
AND THE DAY SO FINE
PENNSYLVANIA TOWNS
SORT OF SLIP RIGHT BY
IN A SOFT LINE SOUTH
UNDER PURPLE SKIES

I WAS DRIVING HOME
THROUGH THE SUNDAY BELLS
THROUGH THE TRAILER TOWNS
THROUGH THE ROLLING HILLS
FROM BEHIND SOME CLOUD
THE SUN STILL SHINES
AND THE STREAMS RUN DOWN
THE MOUNTAIN SIDES

SLOW DOWN WHAT'S THE HURRY THERE'S NO RUSH
DRIVING HOME
TODAY THERE WON'T BE TOO MANY DAYS LIKE TODAY

I WAS DRIVIN' HOME
ON THE BLACK TOP TAR
UP AND DOWN THIS ROAD
LIKE A CARTOON CAR
MASON-DIXON LINE
SLIPS BEHIND ME NOW
GOLDEN FIELDS GO BY
GOLDEN SUN GOES DOWN

Cheryl Wheeler

Gail Vick (Annie) Barnhardt

MEOW

Straightenin' out your back legs, stretching in
   my arms
Yawning, blinking, curling back around
Your dismissive glances slap me back
   somehow
Meow, meow, meow

Sleepin' on the big bed, the sultan slips the scene
Chasing something running in your dream
I am so enchanted, with your twitch and growl
Meow, meow, meow

I see you in Memphis on the Nile in the spring
Swinging through some palace doing your
   Egyptian king thing

You perceive my function, 24 a day
Is to do, for you, anything you say
Where'd you get that notion? How come I
   kowtow?
Meow, meow, meow, meow, meow, meow
Yeah buddy, meow, meow, meow

Cynthia Rudolph

ALMOST

I'm almost everything you have ever wanted
I'm almost your best dream come true
We fit so perfectly
Oh I almost can't believe
How I'm almost all I need to be

There's something now in your smile
Just this side of distant
And something else just that side of true
This road's so old and worn from
The countless nights I've sworn
Oh I could be all you'd need me to
Almost

I don't know where to go
To find our missing pieces
I sit and stare and wonder where to start
But then I look at you and
I know it can't be true
That something's here pulling us apart

Somedays I wonder how we'll walk this line
Somedays I think I feel your heart in mine
Well underneath the surface
Love isn't ever perfect – heaven knows
So we'll just close that door
Almost

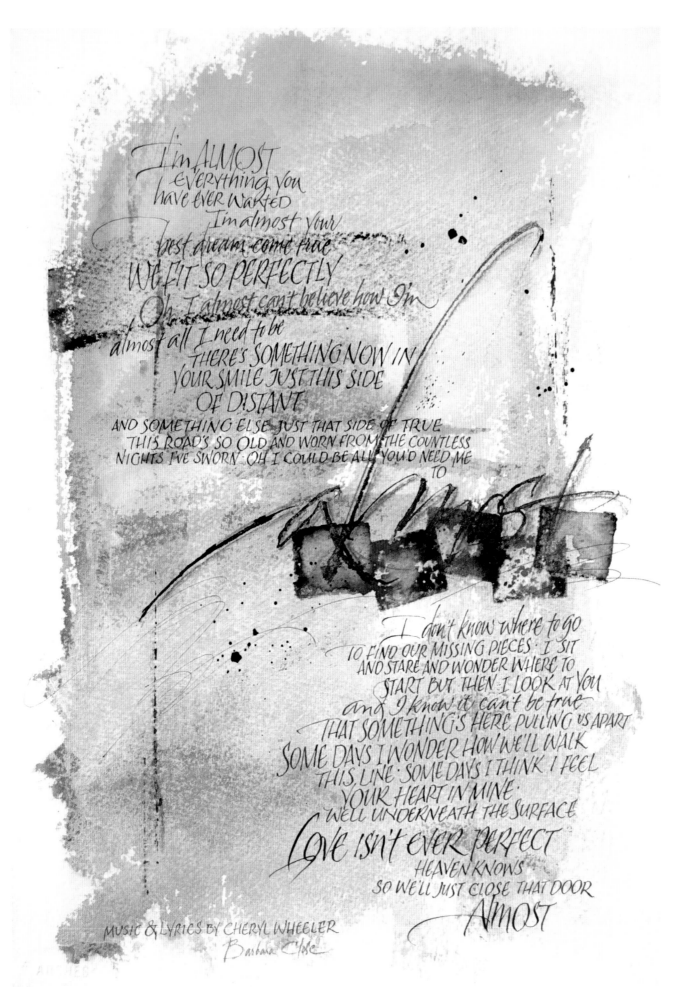

I'm ALMOST
everything you
have ever wanted
I'm almost your
best dream come true
WE FIT SO PERFECTLY
Oh I almost can't believe how I'm
almost all I need to be
THERE'S SOMETHING NOW IN
YOUR SMILE JUST THIS SIDE
OF DISTANT
AND SOMETHING ELSE JUST THAT SIDE OF TRUE
THIS ROAD'S SO OLD AND WORN FROM THE COUNTLESS
NIGHTS I'VE SWORN · OH I COULD BE ALL YOU'D NEED ME
TO

I don't know where to go
TO FIND OUR MISSING PIECES · I SIT
AND STARE AND WONDER WHERE TO
START BUT THEN I LOOK AT YOU
and I know it can't be true
THAT SOMETHING'S HERE PULLING US APART
SOME DAYS I WONDER HOW WE'LL WALK
THIS LINE · SOME DAYS I THINK I FEEL
YOUR HEART IN MINE ·
WELL UNDERNEATH THE SURFACE
Love isn't ever perfect
HEAVEN KNOWS
SO WE'LL JUST CLOSE THAT DOOR
Almost

MUSIC & LYRICS BY CHERYL WHEELER
Barbara Close

Barbara Close

6

POINTING AT THE SUN

Speeding, sailing, spinning through the firmament
And the firmament is speeding somewhere too
So beautiful the mystery, we gaze aloft in wonder
At all the pieces we can see,
  at all the stars we're under

And here on earth we praise what God has done
Every church proclaims the only one
Ants and elephants have lives to run
And all the plants are pointing at the sun

Who and what and where and why
  and how and when
I don't have a whisper of a clue
Do fishes ever look beyond the tank they're in
And somehow contemplate creation too?
I don't expect to understand,
  the question's so beyond us
The mystery is majesty, humbling and wondrous

And here on earth we praise what God has done
Every church proclaims the only one
Ants and elephants have lives to run
And all the plants are pointing at the sun

If atoms zip around too fast for us to see
If somewhere we are zipping that way too
Then some colossal junior high school nerd might be
Adding one to one and getting two
Through eyes the size of galaxies,
  blinking once an eon
He's pondering a particle big enough to be on

And here on earth we praise what God has done
Every church proclaims the only one
Ants and elephants have lives to run
And all the plants are pointing at the sun

Gwen Weaver

ARROW

I wish I could fall in love
though it only leads to trouble, oh I know it does
Still I'd fool myself and gladly, just to feel I was
in love, in love

Wish I could feel my heartbeat rise
and gaze into some gentle, warm, excited eyes
and give myself as truly as an arrow flies
in windless skies

Oh I remember you in the TV light
holding you close to me where we lay
Now I wish I knew some of those softer nights
Whispering quietly, feeling you turn to me

Only last night in the winter dark
I dreamed of how you loved in all your innocence
and I've never known a softer warmer feeling since
or a truer heart

Maybe these dreams are leading me
maybe love is not as gentle as my memory
Maybe time and wishful half-remembered fantasy
are the greatest part

Oh I remember you in the TV light
holding you close to me where we lay
Now I wish I knew some of those softer nights
Whispering quietly, feeling you turn to me

Wish I could feel my heartbeat rise
and gaze into some gentle, warm excited eyes
and give myself as truly as an arrow flies
in windless skies

I wish I could fall in love
Though it only leads to trouble, oh I know it does
Still I'd fool myself and gladly just to feel I was
in love

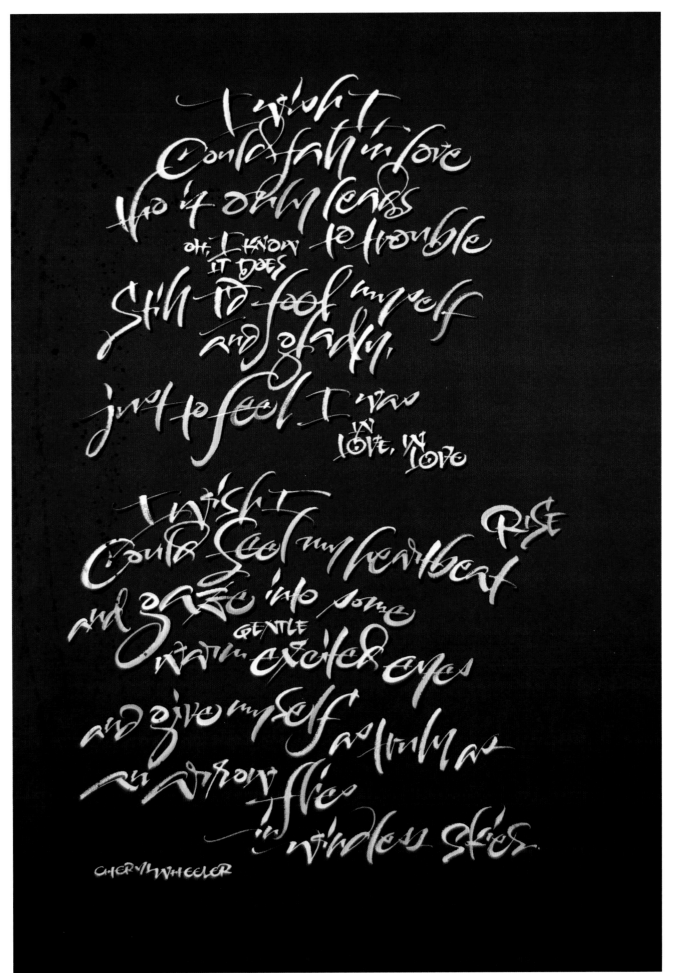

I wish I
could fall in love
if only for a few
oh, I know it's trouble
it does
still to fool myself
and of my
just to feel I was
in
love, in love

I wish I
could steel my heartbeat   rise
and gaze into some
gentle
warm excited eyes
and give myself
an arrow flies
in windless skies.

CHERYL WHEELER

Carl Rohrs

75 SEPTEMBERS

In the year of the yellow cab
Shadow of the great world war
The third kid grandmom had
Came into this world
On a rolling farm in Maryland
When Wilson was the president
As summer blew her goodbye through the trees

Child of changing times
Growing up between the wars
Fords rolled off the lines
And bars all closed their doors
and I imagine you back then
With snap brim hat and farmer's tan
Where horses drew their wagons through the fields

Now the fields are all four lanes
and the moon's not just a name
Are you more amazed at how things change
Or how they stay the same?
And do you sit here on this porch and wonder
How the time flies by,
Or does it seem to barely creep along
With 75 Septembers come and gone?

Were the fields all gold and fawn
Was the spring house dark and cool?
Did the rooster crow at dawn
When they got you up for school?
And would you tell me once again
The tales of granddad's hired men,
And how they drove the old dirt road to town?

'Cause now the fields are all four lanes
And the moon's not just a name
Are you more amazed at how things change
Or how they stay the same?
And do you sit here on this porch and wonder
How the time flies by,
Or does it seem to barely creep along
With 75 Septembers come and gone?

In the year of the yellow cab
Shadow of the great world war.

In the year of the yellow cab
Shadow of a GREAT WORLD WAR
Third kid Grandpop had
came into this world
On a rolling farm in Maryland
when Wilson was
the president

A child of changing times
Growing up between the wars
FORDS rolled off lines, and bar & all
And I imagine you back then
with SNAP BRIM HAT
and FARMERS
CLOSED their DOORS
where horses drew their wagons
through the FIELDS

ARE you MORE AMAZED at HOW THIN GS

AS summer blew her GOODBYE through the TREES

and DO YOU SIT HERE on this PORCH and WONDER HOW the TIME FLIES BY

or DOES IT SEEM to BARELY CREEP ALONG with 75 SEPTEMBERS

CHANGE or HOW they STAY THE SAME

Now the fields are all four lanes
And the moon's not just a name
CHANGE or How the things
And DO YOU
SIT HERE on this PORCH and WONDER
HOW the TIME FLIES BY or DOES IT
seem to barely creep ALONG the SAME
75 SEPTEMBERS
COME and GONE
come and gone

Were the fields all GOLD and fawn
Was the SPRING HOUSE dark and cool
Did the rooster crow at dawn
When they got you off to SCHOOL
And WOULD you tell me one again the TALES of GRANDADS
And how they drove the OLD DIRT ROAD
to TOWN
WITH 75 SEPTEMBERS come and GONE

WORDS BY CHERYL WHEELER
SCRIPSIT PATTE LEATHE
2009

Patte Leathe

12

HOLDING ON

I won't let you fall. Hear me loud and clear
I will not let go. I will be right here, holding on

What's that someone said
   of a closed and opened door?
Brighter days ahead,
   look that way while you're holding on
 Holding on, holding on

And when some lonesome wind has hemmed you in
Don't you believe that sound
You will surely rise above these tides
To higher ground

With the past not far behind
   and the future not in stone
I suppose from time to time
   we'll be howling at the moon
And holding on

But I won't let you fall. Hear me loud and clear
I will not let go. I will be right here, holding on
Holding on, holding on

I WON'T
LET YOU FALL

HOLDING ON

HEAR
ME LOUD
AND
CLEAR
I WILL
NOT LET GO
I WILL
BE RIGHT
HERE
HOLDING
ON

What's that someone said of a closed and opened door
Brighter days ahead look that way while you're
holding on holding on holding on

When some lonesome wind has hemmed you in
don't you believe that sound
You will surely rise above these tides to higher ground

With the past not far behind and the future not in stone
I suppose from time to time we'll be howling at the moon and
holding on

CHERYL WHEELER

Jane Parillo

14

ACES

My old friend - you said to me
I ain't bein' what I'm supposed to be
Well I don't know - it could be true
I know I wasn't always there for you

Now you're ready to walk out - you're ready to run
Talk to me, can't you see
I would never wanna do what it seems I've done
You can't deal me the aces and think I wouldn't play
Don't let this be the reason you would walk away

The things you think - that I should do
I've never understood that part of you
I know I've tried to be your friend
But you feel undermined and hurt again

Now don't let it convince you - don't take it to heart
Compromise realize you can never really run everything you start
You can't deal me the aces and think I wouldn't play
Don't let this be the reason you would walk away

I guess I said I couldn't see
How things could turn out like they've come to be
If I lied - if I knew
I was only tryin' to think of you

Now don't let it convince you - don't take it to heart
Compromise realize you can never really run everything you start
You can't deal me the aces and think I wouldn't play
Don't let this be the reason you would walk away

Now you're ready to walk out - you're ready to run
Talk to me, can't you see
I would never wanna do what it seems I've done
You can't deal me the aces and think I wouldn't play
Don't let this be the reason you would walk away

YOU CAN'T DEAL ME THE ACES
AND THINK I WOULDN'T PLAY
DON'T LET THIS BE THE REASON
YOU WOULD WALK AWAY

YOU CAN'T
DEAL ME
THE
ACES

Gemma Black

16

QUARTER MOON

And they seem to know each other very well
They speak across the garden and not a soul could tell
They can read the summer sky
and hear the back brook swell
And they seem to know each other very well

And they drive up north on Sunday afternoons
And he buys her wooden windmills
 and whales and quarter moons
She feeds the birds all winter
   and she knows them by their tunes
And they drive up north on Sunday afternoons

All summer long, they make the garden grow
Keep the green so strong
Oh, wish them well, for standing on their own

And they buried their old dog in their backyard
With a fence and plastic roses,
   and St. Francis standing guard
She speaks of him quite often, to this day she takes it hard
And they buried their old dog in their backyard

And she brings me plants and flowers all the time
We dig the holes together,
   but she has to help with mine
When she pats the soil around them,
   oh my God, her eyes can shine
And she brings me plants and flowers all the time

And they speak about their lives as almost gone
Waiting for the sunset from an old and distant dawn
Selling off the land except the part they're living on
And they speak about their lives as almost gone

And they seem to know each other very well
They speak across the garden and not a soul could tell
They can read the summer sky
   and hear the back brook swell
And they seem to know each other very well

Quarter Moon

And they seem to know each other very well
They speak across the garden and not a soul could tell
They can read the summer sky
    and they can hear the back brook swell
And they seem to know each other very well

And they drive up north on sunday afternoons
And he buys her wooden windmills
    and whales and quarter moons
She feeds the birds all winter
    and she knows them by their tunes
And they drive up north on sunday afternoons

And all summer long,
    they make the garden grow
Keep the green so strong
Oh, wish them well,
    for standing on their own

And they speak about their lives as almost gone
Waiting for the sunset from an old and distant dawn
Selling off the land except the part they're living on
And they speak of their lives as almost gone

And they seem to know each other very well
They speak across the garden and not a soul could tell
They can read the summer sky
    and they can hear the back brook swell
And they seem to know each other very well

LYRICS BY CHERYL WHEELER

Elissa Barr 2010

Elissa Barr

18

SPRING

There's a thaw beneath the fallen snow
And the geese don't know which way to go
There's a warm wind blowin' round the bend
And the days are growin' long again

And I will go down by the river
Wash the cold away
Gaze across the water, all day

There's a bird rehearsing on a wire
And a soft green underneath the briar
There's a hazy ring around the moon
And the rains of spring are comin' soon

And I will sail out over the ocean
Stare down into the sea
Feel the warm salty wind of salvation blowin' through me

And I been down for too long baby
And I been up all night
I know it - I hear it
I think maybe
It's gonna be alright

There's a wing just waiting for a chance
And a yellow blossom on a branch
There's a warm wind blowin' 'round the bend
And the days are growin' long again

And I will sail out over the ocean
stare down into the sea
Feel the warm salty wind of salvation
blowin' through me.

— CHERYL WHEELER

Kristen Doty

RAINY ROAD INTO ATLANTA

Rainy road into Atlanta, time is truly crawlin' by
Drops of rain on my side window, nothin', nothin' on my mind
Driving through the old horizon though it never seems that way
Clouds are rolling through these skies in fifty thousand shades of grey

Always on the move is a mesmerizing groove
It's a quiet call, it's a trance to fall into

Texaco and exit only, Grandma Peaches Cafe
Bridges freeze before the roadway, I don't think they will today
Single seating at the counter. How can I be here again?
Filthy shirt construction worker with Georgia on his face and hands

Always on the move is a mesmerizing groove
In an April rain as the Southern spring comes through

I don't know where the winter went, but summertime is closing in
If bloom and shoot is what they meant, I'd say the south just rose again
How beautiful these roads I wander, all these towns I'm passing through
Oh blessed is this weary traveler, finally coming home to you

RAINY ROAD INTO ATLANTA,
TIME IS TRULY CRAWLIN' BY.
DROPS OF RAIN ON MY SIDE WINDOW,
NOTHIN', NOTHIN' ON MY MIND
DRIVING THROUGH THE OLD HORIZON
THOUGH IT NEVER SEEMS THAT WAY
CLOUDS ARE ROLLING THROUGH
THESE SKIES IN FIFTY THOUSAND
SHADES OF GREY.

ALWAYS ON THE MOVE IS A
MESMERIZING GROOVE
IT'S A QUIET CALL
IT'S A CHANCE TO FALL INTO

TEXACO AND EXIT ONLY,
GRANDMA PEACHES CAFE
BRIDGES FREEZE BEFORE
THE ROADWAY, I DON'T THINK
THEY WILL TODAY. SINGLE SEATING
AT THE COUNTER. HOW CAN I BE HERE
AGAIN? FILTHY SHIRT CONSTRUCTION
WORKER WITH GEORGIA ON
HIS FACE AND HANDS.

I DON'T KNOW WHERE THE
WINTER WENT, BUT SUMMERTIME
IS CLOSING IN. IF BLOOM AND SHOOT
IS WHAT THEY MEANT, I'D SAY THE SOUTH
JUST ROSE AGAIN. HOW BEAUTIFUL
THESE ROADS I WANDER, ALL THESE TOWNS
I'M PASSING THROUGH. OH BLESSED IS
THIS WEARY TRAVELER.

FINALLY COMING HOME TO YOU" by Cheryl Wheeler

Maureen Squires

22

BEYOND THE LIGHTS

Thought you'd bide your time and play your part
    but you were wrong dear
Somewhere down the line your lonely heart
    could not belong here
And in some frame of reason, beyond our vision,
Your love lagged behind and fell apart
Without a soul to hear

On a night like this the stars don't shine
    and there's no moonlight
We're like you I guess, we bide our time,
    try to play our parts right
    and wonder where you gathered your angry sorrow
Through the rolling mist the scenes unwind
They seem so clear tonight

And in my sleep you are crying still
The way you touch your brow, hang your head
I never knew and I never will
The voices haunting you, a thing that I could do.

Were they in your stars
    those lonely nights, tormented hours?
Something snapped your spars
    and slacked your lines and took your powers
Did no one see you sinking till you'd gone under?
While you slipped so far beyond the lights,
    were we just watching ours?

Marta Legeckis

24

SUMMER'S ALMOST OVER

Summer's almost over and I'm crying but I don't know why
Sentimental old fool, weeping for this blue, blue sky
And the way the cat is sleeping and the way the
 garden grew
Wagging dogs who lick my face and the way I feel for you

Paddling in the kayaks, with my sister,
 through the quiet creek
Moon upon the water and the river breeze upon my cheek
And the way my Father shuffles with his courage
 and his cane
And the way September bluffs and feints till autumn
 falls again
Summer's almost over and I'm crying but I don't know why

A party for my birthday and a tractor for my 50 years
Swallows at their bird play spin and dive above the new
 mown fields
And a week in Colorado, reading books with my best friend
And the thing I knew I couldn't do and now I know I can

Who could help but welcome autumn and the promise
 of the winter snow?
Still there's something sweet and wistful as I watch this
 lovely summer go
But the sun is sinking sooner and the weeds have won at last
With the berries on the bushes and the crickets in the grass
Summer's almost over and I'm crying but I don't know why

Summer's almost over and I'm crying but I don't know why
  Sentimental old fool, weeping for this blue, blue sky
And the way the cat is sleeping and the way the garden grew
  Wagging dogs who lick my face and the way I feel for you

Paddling in the kayaks with my sister, through the quiet creek
  Moon upon the water and the river breeze upon my cheek
And the way my father shuffles with his courage and his cane
And the way September blurs and feints till autumn falls again

Oh summer's almost over and I'm crying
            and I don't know why

A party for my birthday and a tractor for my 50 years
  Swallows at their bird play spin and dive above the new mown fields
And a week in Colorado reading books with my best friend
  And the thing I knew I couldn't do and now I know I can
Who could help but welcome autumn and the promise of winter snow
  Still there's something sweet and wistful as I watch this lovely summer go
But the sun is sinking sooner and the weeds have won at last
  With the berries on the bushes and the crickets in the grass
Oh Summer's almost over and I'm crying but I don't know why
                              Cheryl Wheeler

Annie Cicale

LIGHTING UP THE MIGHTY MISSISSIPPI

Big yellow moon, dark blue sky
Lighting up the mighty Mississippi
I'm headed home, I can't decide
If my heart is just too full or just too empty
Through the thousands of miles of the rivers and hills
And the highways I've come to know so well
I always knew I could fall back on you
Now it wouldn't matter which way I fell

Still it's nice to keep movin', down the dotted line
Past the tractors in their amber waves of grain
If I keep my eyes open, take a little time
No two towns will ever look the same
And sometimes on the AM radio
I get a little local Polka show
And folks are friendly everywhere I go

Drank too much in Dayton, paid the whole next day
The snow in South Dakota was so dry it blew away
And it's not like someone's waitin' when I get home anyway
So I leave for Portland pretty soon, then down through Monterey
But right now this big old yellow moon is filling up the sky
And lighting up the mighty Mississippi

Nancy Galligan

UNDERBRUSH

Let me lift this burden from you
Let me take this pain from you
Let me always be the one to
Hear you, see you, pull you through

How could I have been so thoughtless
How could I have failed to see
Every day's a work in progress
Every page a mystery

This is nothing but the daily grumble roaring
Nothing but the sweep we need so much
Now we got a snowy Sunday morning
And we've already cleared the underbrush,
   the underbrush

No regrets, no road not taken
Nothing I would rather do
Some days we can lose our faith in
Every thing we thought we knew

You're the light on all my pages
Oh my love, my even keel
And any words I use to say this
Pale before the way I feel

This is nothing but the daily grumble roaring
Nothing but the sweep we need so much
Now we got a snowy Sunday morning
And we've already cleared the underbrush,
   the underbrush

Maybe there's a rhythm here, a sort of ebb and flow
Every orbit varies over time I guess
Disappearing down the trail,
   the dogs kick up the snow
Given our good fortune, we can do no less

This is nothing but the daily grumble roaring
Nothing but the sweep we need so much
Now we got a snowy Sunday morning
And we've already cleared the underbrush,
   the underbrush

this
IS
NOTHING
BUT
THE
DAILY
GRUMBLE
ROARING
NOTHING
BUT
THE
SWEEP
WE
NEED
SO MUCH
NOW
WE
GOT A
SNOWY SUNDAY
MORNING
AND WE'VE
ALREADY
CLEARED
THE
UNDERBRUSH

Let me lift this burden
from you
Let me take this pain
from you
Let me always be the
one to
Hear you, see you,
pull you through

How could I have
been so thoughtless
How could I have
failed to see
Every day's a work
in progress
Every page a mystery

No regrets, no road
not taken
Nothing I would
rather do
Some days we can
lose our faith in
Every thing
we thought
we knew

You're the light on
all my pages
Oh my love, my
even keel
And any words
I use to say this
Pale before the
way I feel

Maybe there's
a rhythm here,
a sort of ebb and
flow
Every orbit varies
over time I guess
Disappearing down
the trail,
the dogs
kick up the snow
Given
our good
fortune
we
can do
no
less.

CHERYL WHEELER

Gerry Jackson Kerdok

LITTLE KIDS

Hello come in great to see you again
Been such a long drive guess you're beat
Heavens! What's that? It's a dwarf in a hat
Oh no you've brought the children how sweet

I'm sure you mentioned it when we'd last spoken
Let me just move these so they don't get broken
He's such a delight
And you're staying the night
You know I just love little kids

Little kids are sticky and cute
Little kids have mud on their boots
And they run through my house
And they torment my dogs
And I surely do love little kids

Let's sit in here honey this is your chair
No kitty's afraid when you shout
Oh it's okay it was old anyway
and the other one washes right out

Don't touch the parrot That's right it's a mean one
How do they do it? I'd need a machine gun
She's patient and kind I'd be out of my mind
You know I just love little kids

Little kids will cry anywhere
Little kids have food in their hair
And they run through my house and they torment my dogs
And I surely do love little kids

Don't pull their tails No they're not mean
Yes if they bite you it hurts
It's just a sears coffee machine
Nobody knows how it works

The company's gone and I'm sitting alone
Away from the noise and the fuss
The pets have returned and this weekend I've learned
little children are nothing like us

They put their food in ridiculous places
They leave their fingerprints on their own faces
Oh how could you say we all started this way?
You know I just love little kids
Little kids get up way before me
Little kids leave a trail of debris
And they run through my house and they torment my dogs
And I surely do love little kids

I just love little kids

Little kids will cry anywhere. Little kids are sticky and cute. Little kids are good on their own. Little kids have cried in their food on their mom. I sincerely do love little kids own faces their fingerprints on their dogs. And then they leave for a moment. And then I love little Kids. And they run through in ridiculous places. They put their food as they run through my house.

"Little Kids" - lyrics by Cheryl Wheeler scripsit Katherine Malmsten 2010

Katherine Malmsten

32

MRS. PINOCCI'S GUITAR

Diane and Billy been friends forever
They go back a long time
They grew up together
She called to tell us
He'd written from Rome
For the whole month of August
He'd be at home

So we went to see him
At her house one evening
In the place where they'd spent
all their summers as kids
We walked all around
In the small bayside town
Where his Dad's called the bingo
for thirty-five years

And later on that night
Under the porch light
Mrs. Pinocci brought her six string over
She said she'd been playin'
since she turned fifty-seven
And now I guess she's more than
twenty years older

She played Yankee Doodle,
we sang along with her
She passed it around
and we all played a number
Neighbors and friends
dropped by for the singin'
And later a guy no one knew
came to sit in

For the moon on the water
For the light from the stars
Oh I thank the spirits
Whatever they are
For friendships that last
And songs from the past
And Mrs. Pinocci's guitar

DIANE AND BILLY BEEN FRIENDS FOREVER THEY GO BACK A
LONG TIME THEY GREW UP TOGETHER SHE CALLED TO TELL
US HE'D WRITTEN FROM ROME FOR THE WHOLE MONTH
OF AUGUST HE'D BE AT HOME

SO WE WENT TO SEE HIM AT HER HOUSE
ONE EVENING IN THE PLACE WHERE
THEY'D SPENT ALL THEIR SUMMERS AS
KIDS WE WALKED ALL AROUND IN THE
SMALL BAY SIDE TOWN WHERE HIS
DAD'S CALLED THE BINGO FOR 35 YEARS

AND LATER ON THAT NIGHT UNDER
THE PORCH LIGHT MRS. PINOCCI
BROUGHT HER SIX STRING OVER SHE
SAID SHE'D BEEN PLAYING SINCE SHE
TURNED 57 AND NOW I GUESS SHE'S
MORE THAN TWENTY YEARS OLDER

SHE PLAYED YANKEE DOODLE WE SANG
ALONG WITH HER SHE PASSED IT AROUND
AND WE ALL PLAYED A NUMBER NEIGHBORS
AND FRIENDS DROPPED BY FOR A LITTLE SINGIN'
THEN LATER A GUY NO ONE KNEW CAME TO SIT IN

For the Moon on the Water
For the Light from the Stars
Oh I thank the spirits whatever they are
For friendships that last
Songs from the past
and Mrs. Pinocci's Guitar

Lyrics by Cheryl Wheeler

Toni Kelly

34

SILVER LINING

Hard times came, we fell out, then we fell back in
Missed our strokes, lost our stride, didn't know where we'd been
Found ourselves on opposite shores, who knows how we did
I don't even care anymore – gonna just look ahead

And I'm gonna be your certain silver lining
I'm gonna be your lullaby at night
I'm gonna be your baby alright

Now we know we held on, sailing in seas so rough
Swells so deep, winds so strong- couldn't quite capsize us
Wish I knew some formula now- had some guarantee
You can count on trouble once in a while
And baby you can count on me

'Cause I'm gonna be your certain silver lining
I'm gonna be your lullaby at night
I'm gonna be your baby alright

Every night - now hear this
Cross my heart-read my lips
Everyday- right and wrong
Unconditionally I know

I'm gonna be your certain silver lining
I'm gonna be your lullaby at night
I'm gonna be your baby alright

Lisa Engelbrecht

LITTLE LONELY THING

No reason I guess
No dark and troubled time
Just a loneliness
some traveler left behind
And it had no place to be
So it crept inside of me
But I don't mind

It nestled right in
just to hang its head and cry
For the cold north wind
For the wide, white, winter sky
There'll be no brave face to keep
till it's cried itself to sleep
So I won't try

And when it wakes up I'll explain
How winter always leads to spring
How even when our skies are blue
we need a little lonely too
To keep our hearts stretched open wide
To touch the edge of either side

So I'll keep it right here
This little lonely thing
I'll lend my ear
Be kind and comforting
It's the least that I can do
Because I've been lonely too
Lonely too

No reason I guess
No dark and troubled time
Just a loneliness
some traveler left behind

little lonely thing words & music by cheryl wheeler
no reason i guess no dark and troubled time
just a loneliness some traveler left behind and it had
no place to go so it crept inside me out i don't mind
i held her right in just to hold its head and cry for the
cold north wind or the wide white winter sky there'll
be no brave ... face to ... tossed by its
cried the ... to sleep so
i won't ... try and
when ... it wakes
i ex ... din
now ... inter
and i ... stars
ends ... to sort
now e ... when
in ow ... sky are
o we we ... need a
ttle on ... ey too
to keep our ... hearts
stretched ... opened
wide to tou ... other
edge of either ... side so i
keep it north ... ere this ttle
lonely thing i'll ... lend my ear
only be kind and ... comforting its
the least i can do be ... cause i've been
lonely lonely too lonely i do no reason i guess no
dark and troubled time just a loneliness
some song traveler left behind. words and music
by cheryl wheeler. a loneliness. ttle lonely thing

Jen Grove

38

WHEEL ON A WIRE

It don't seem to matter how the evenings go
For that morning sun comes slowly along
The day brings back the distance and wipes the mood away
Like all the stars who couldn't stay after the dawn

And I'm like a wheel on a wire
Speeding along the track
Traveling too fast for lookin' back
And I can't see

So one more cup of coffee in a ragged afternoon
Seeing the sun beneath the moon I drift away
And out among the shadows, the passion comes to rise
In all the pairs of hungry eyes whose glances stray

And I'm like a wheel on a wire
Burning along the track
Traveling too fast for lookin' back
And I can't see
I feel like a wheel on a wire
Speeding beyond control
Bated and breathless I feel my soul
Spin out of me.

Myrna Rosen

40

BLUE SUMMER DAY

The cats are lyin' in the yard next door and they turn me a sleepy eye,
roll in the grass and spring so fast for a lazy butterfly
And it's a blue summer day
Breezes blow and curtains sway
A newcomer, blue summer day

The felines file to the backyard fence and they crouch in a lethal row
Blue jays flee from the apple tree, bees buzz to and fro
And it's a blue summer day
Clotheslines hung in a hundred shades
A newcomer, blue summer day

A loud lawn mower in a lawn somewhere brings a mem'ry to my ear
From the past I smell the grass and see the green so clear
And it's a blue summer day
Spiders spin and pipers play
A newcomer, blue summer day

When the lawns are mowed and the laundry's stowed and the dusk is drawing near
We'll light the torches on our porches and drink ourselves a beer
'Cause it's a blue summer day
With streaks of red and hints of gray
A newcomer, blue summer day
It is a true wonder blue summer day

Mike Gold

Detail

WALK AROUND DOWNTOWN

Let's go downtown and walk around tonight
Let's go sit across some table and feel lucky
You will point out something perfect in this light
Come on, come on, let's go walk around
Come on, come on, let's go walk around

Yes, I see now, though I never did before
how these steeples in this sky line look so lovely
I am bowled down and couldn't love you more
Come on, come on, let's go walk around
Come on, come on, let's go walk around

This summer night we are wandering through
Is perfect in this Providence July
These city lights really shine on you
And I should know, 'cause darlin' so do I

So let's go downtown and walk around tonight
where the river flows among the stony bridges
Till the dark comes, and it really hasn't quite
Come on, come on, let's go walk around
Come on, come on, let's go walk around

L et's go downtown and walk around tonight
Let's go sit around some table and feel lucky
You will point out something perfect in this light
Come on, come on, let's go walk around.

Yes, I see now, though I never did before
How these steeples in this skyline look so lovely
I am bowled down
and I couldn't love you more
Come on, come on, let's go walk around.

This summer night
we are wandering through
Is perfect in this Providence July
These city lights really shine on you
And I should know
'cause darlin' so do I.

So let's go downtown and walk around tonight
Where the river flows among the stony bridges
Till the dark comes and it really hasn't quite
Come on, come on, let's go walk around.

...come on, come on, let's go walk around... ...come on, come on, let's go walk around.

WALK AROUND DOWNTOWN *Lyrics:* CHERYL WHEELER *Calligraphy & Design:* JAN BOYD

Jan Boyd

SINCE YOU'VE BEEN GONE

A woman my age, sittin' here cryin'
I ought to be stronger than I am
Ought to take comfort from wisdom or somethin' like that.
But it isn't that way, 'cause sooner or later
I'm still that nervous ninth grader
Watching you pull us together, I never knew how

And since you've been gone I'm just fallin' apart
There's a hole in my life, in my soul, in my heart
And I stare out this window till light becomes dark
And there's nothing that's touching me now

But not to complain, we're just bereft, not deserted
Lord knows your rest was deserved
It's just your absence is present in all that I do
In the sun on the field, in the poem I keep saying
In the hymn that some church bells were playing
You have always been part of them but I never knew

And since you've been gone I'm just fallin' apart
There's a hole in my life, in my soul, in my heart
And I stare out this window till light becomes dark
And there's nothing that's touching me now

How could I ever begin to say
Surely you already knew
What is this world with you gone away
How can this finally be true

And since you've been gone I'm just fallin' apart
There's a hole in my life, in my soul, in my heart
And I stare out this window till light becomes dark
And there's nothing that's touching me now

A woman my age,
 sittin' here cryin'
I ought to be stronger than I am
 Ought to take comfort
from wisdom or somethin' like that
 But it isn't that way
  'cause sooner or later
I'm still that nervous 9th grader
watching you pull us together,
 I never knew how

And since you've been gone
 I'm just falling apart
There's a hole in my life, in my soul,
  in my heart
And I stare out this window
 till light becomes dark
And there's nothing that's touching
 me now

IT'S
JUST
YOUR
ABSENCE
IS
PRESENT
IN
ALL THAT
I DO

But not to complain,
 we're just bereft, not deserted
Lord knows your rest was deserved
It's just your absence is present
  in all that I do
In the sun on the field, in the poem —
 I keep saying
In the hymn that some church bells
 were playing
You have always been part of them
 but I never knew

How could I ever begin to say
 Surely you already knew
What is this world with you gone away
How can this finally be true

WORDS AND MUSIC BY CHERYL WHEELER, 2004

Jane Parillo

YOUR GOD

Is your God the same God who's working with the Pope?
Is it the same God suspicious of Tinky Winky?
Is it the God corralling virgins into herds of 72,
deciding where to send them when the glorious martyrs are through?

Is your God the same God who's burning the science books
and trampling lives to hoist the right to life signs?
Or is He running the breeding program from the Temple by the lake
till one big inbred family will be an entire state?

Are they His priests who can't keep from buggering little boys?
Is your cash retaining their attorneys?
I guess He had to overlook the nastiness with the tykes,
to keep the grace of marriage from the clutches of fags and dykes

Is your God the same God who won the Superbowl?
I hope it's not that loser God the Eagles had
Or is yours the God decreeing all the women wear a sack,
and presiding over stonings and beheadings in Iraq?

Is your God commanding you
to tell everybody what to do,
to kill your brain, praise his name
bury the bastard who's not the same,
spew your heinous and hateful shit
like something holy was driving it
to take over all the earth and skies above?
Oh mercy, whatever happened to the GOD of love?

J. Daniel Mooney

I SEE YOUR EYES

We've been out of control and over the line
Under the sway of indecision
Keepin' it goin' and we don't know why anymore
If there's something to lose and something to
  gain, is it a no win situation?
We've been confusin' passion and pain
And she says we both keep score

But she's so angry and she don't want me
the way you do
I don't wanna just jump the gun
over something new
But oh I think of you

I see your eyes in my dreams
I see you face in my sleep
I hear your voice talk to me
And I can't hear myself speak
When I see your eyes

Whatever it took we couldn't explain
We don't know how to make it better
Remembering looks we haven't exchanged
  for so long
Maybe we got no reason to stay,
She says she's alone when we're together
And sometimes I wonder if we're so afraid
We're just holdin' on

Julie Gray

HIS HOMETOWN

When he was a boy, sittin' in school
Starin' out the window at the fields he knew
All that he wanted was to be there too
Drivin' his tractor through the morning dew

Dust from the sun, mud from the rain
It felt like an honor to him all the same
And it's the simplest thing, he's a self taught man
He loves his work because he loves the land

And he can change the hills, plant the trees
Dig the wells, spread the seeds
Mow the fields, plow the streets
In his hometown

The seasons roll by, year into year.
He's worked all his life and he's worked right here
The winters go slow if the snows don't come
But it's soon to be summer when the tractors hum

And he can change the hills, plant the trees
Dig the wells, spread the seeds
Mow the fields, plow the streets
In his hometown

I've seen him do things I just can't believe
Makes gentle giants of those big machines
He moves a boulder like a paper bag
And he moves a tree like it was all he had

Blessed is the soul who has truly found
Something to rest on while the world turns round
I think he'd say this is how he feels
When the dark earth is turning underneath his
 wheels

And he can change the hills, plant the trees
Dig the wells, spread the seeds
Mow the fields, plow the streets
In his hometown

Thomas Hoyer

52

TIME TAKETH AWAY

Time takes us from cradle to grave
From helpless to helpless again
And there ain't no turning back
On this one way track
'Cause one day we're bound to give in

And it just keeps rollin' by
Like the sun in the sky
Like the darkness
that follows the day
And it may be the Lord who giveth
But it's time that taketh away

You watch us grow up
We watch you grow old
It's the order we've known
from the start
But it don't help to know
When time's runnin' low
'Cause I swear it still tears us apart

And it just keeps rollin' by
Like the sun in the sky
Like the darkness
that follows the day
And it may be the Lord who giveth
But it's time that taketh away

And how can I start
To take this in stride?
Who let your strength start to fray?
And how can I stop the
tears in my eyes?
You're fading away, fading away

And it just keeps rollin' by
Like the sun in the sky
Like the darkness
that follows the day
And it may be the Lord who giveth
But it's time that taketh away

music & lyrics by cheryl wheeler • design & lettering by louis l. lemoine

Louis Lemoine

HARD LINE TO DRAW

We been spendin' sleepless nights
Wonderin' what to do
And I don't know if
I can take this
When I look at you

'Cause maybe we're just biding time
Till something comes along
I need to slow down, I don't know now
If this is right or wrong

It's a hard line to draw
Close play to call
These days I just can't say at all
And it's sure not black and white
If the dream is worth the fight
And I hope somehow
We can work this out alright

I know the fire and fascination
Is bound to fade in time
But can it be right
When it seems like
There's nothin' left behind?
We ask ourselves a thousand questions
Wonderin' how'd it come to this
And now I'm not sure
Maybe it's just me or, maybe this is what love is

It's a hard line to draw
Close play to call
These days I just can't say at all

And if love is blind
Then we're a blank stare
Half the time we're goin' nowhere
I'm scared to change now, don't wanna tell you
Scared to find out there's nothin' left to lose

Hard line to draw
Close play to call
Hard line to draw

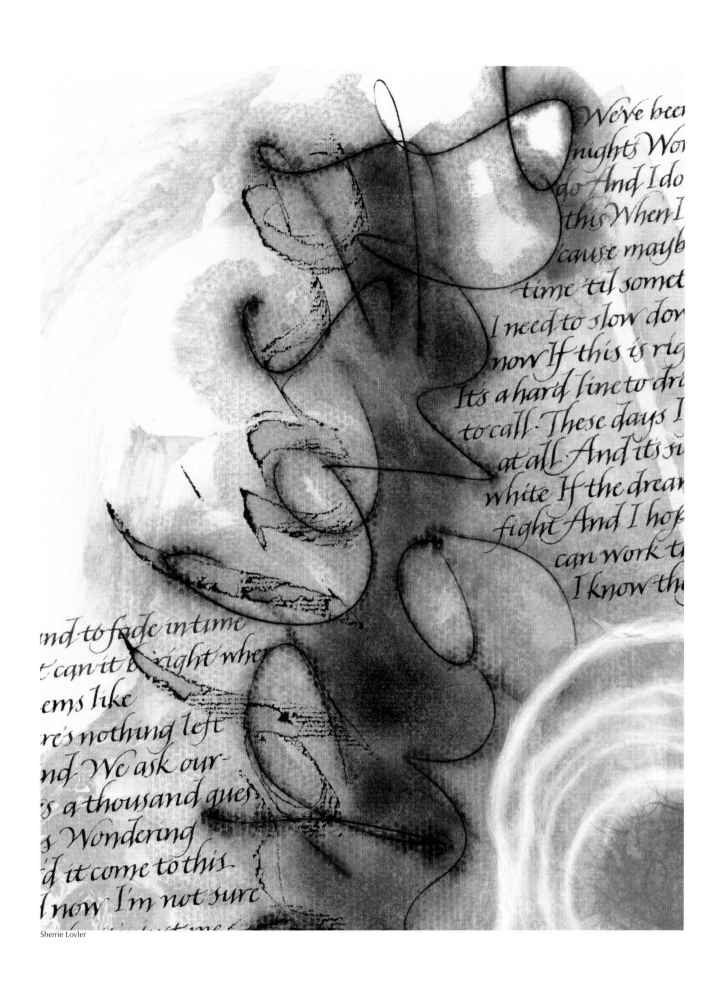

Sherrie Lovler

IS IT PEACE OR IS IT PROZAC?

I'm psychiatric now
It just happened
I don't know how
Life was moving right along
At a reasonable clip
When bang zoom
Lost my grip
And I'm psychiatric now

Oh I might smile
thinking things are really swell
Or I might cry
trouble is you just can't tell
'Cause I'm psychiatric now

So when I'd had enough of this
I went to a psychiatrist
I said I'm acting crazily
I think my mind is gone from me
He looked at me said I agree
You think you're nuts and seem to be
So he prescribed some pills for me
And I went to the pharmacy
I took them and I seemed to be
just ... fine
There's just one little question
on my mind.

Is it peace or is it Prozac?
I don't care
No need to know that
When the moon is full
and the world's too close
I just keep my smile and I up my dose

Is it peace or is it Prozac?
Is this mellow am I a maniac?
Is my mind out there
and can I get it back?
Is it peace I feel or is it Prozac?
Prozac

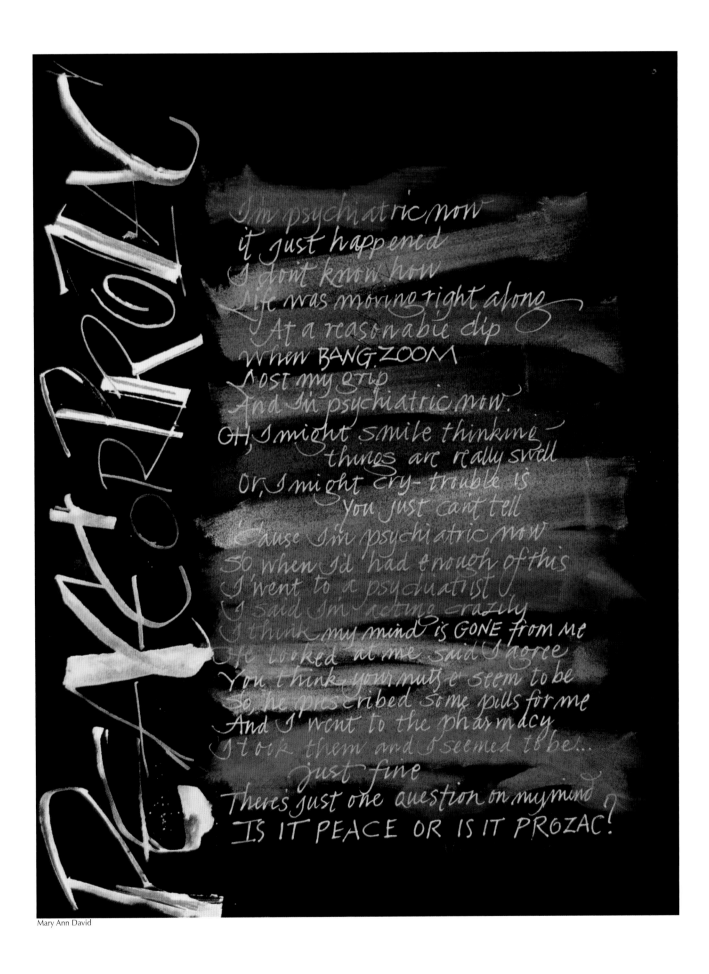

I'm psychiatric now
it just happened
I don't know how
Life was moving right along
At a reasonable clip
When BANG.ZOOM
I lost my grip
And I'm psychiatric now.
OH, I might smile thinking
things are really swell
Or, I might cry - trouble is
You just can't tell
'cause I'm psychiatric now
So when I'd had enough of this
I went to a psychiatrist
I said I'm acting crazily
I think my mind is GONE from me
He looked at me said I agree
You think you nuts e seem to be
So, he prescribed some pills for me
And I went to the pharmacy
I took them and I seemed to be...
just fine
There's just one question on my mind
IS IT PEACE OR IS IT PROZAC?

Mary Ann David

YOU'RE THE ONE

I don't know if it's vast and eternal love
Like they talk about on TV
I don't know if it's all that we're dreamin' of
Or if it was meant to be
But when I'm on the road at night, with poison on my tongue
I close my eyes and thank my stars
Darlin' you're the one

I don't know if it's all that you'll ever need
I don't know what the years will bring
I don't know why you opened your heart to me
After all of my wandering
You took me back, you took me in
When I'd come so undone
I just close my eyes and thank my stars
Darlin' you're the one

And as long as it takes till you find your faith
If you want to believe again
I'll be there, I'll be true, I will see you through
I'll do everything I can
I will not turn and walk away
No matter what should come
I'll just close my eyes and thank my stars
Darlin' you're the one

I don't know if it's vast and eternal love
Like they talk about on TV
I don't know it's all that we dreamin' of
Or if it was meant to be
But when I'm on the road at night with poison on
my tongue
I close my eyes and thank my stars
Darlin' you're the one

I don't know if it's all that you'll ever need
I don't know what the years will bring
I don't know why you opened your heart to me
After all of my wandering
You took me back, you took me in
When I'd come so undone
I just close my eyes and thank my stars
Darlin' you're the one

And as long as it takes till you find your faith
If you want to believe again
I'll be there, I'll be true, I really see you through
I'll do everything I can
I will not turn and walk away
No matter what should come
I'll just close my eyes and thank my stars
Darlin' you're the one

Lyrics and Music by Cheryl Wheeler · Lettering by C.A. Millner

C. A. Millner

GREY AND GREEN

With the blazing sun at bay on this August day
It seems so still, so safe, so serene
Beneath this welcome shroud of heavy cloud
With the world all grey and green

With the world all green and grey
Till the clouds come undone,
   we will hide from the sun
And I'll drink this light with all my might...all day

So let the day go by with the bright blue sky
There's enchantment in this soft and muted scene
When all the leaves appear so lush and clear
In a thousand shades of green

With the world all green and grey
Till the clouds come undone,
   we will hide from the sun
And I'll drink this light with all my might...all day

And when we turn away to end the day
From the brilliant star we never see at night
I will lie in bed and fill my head
With a million shades of light.

WITH THE BLAZING
SUN AT BAY · ON THIS
AUGUST DAY · IT SEEMS
SO STILL, SO SAFE, SO
SERENE · BENEATH
THIS WELCOME SHROUD ·
OF HEAVY CLOUD · WITH
THE WORLD ALL ...

GRAY & GREEN

TILL THE HIDE THE LIGHT · WITH HIS LIGHT ·

SO LET THE DAY
BLUE SKY ·
IN THIS SOFT &
ALL THE LEAVES
CLEAR ·

FROM THE SUN · AND I'LL DRINK ALL DAY. WITH ALL NIGHT · ALL DAY. CLOUDS COME UNDONE · I'LL THE WORLD ALL GREEN & GRAY.

GO BY · WITH THE BRIGHT
THERE'S ENCHANTMENT
MUTED SCENE · WHEN
APPEAR · SO LUSH AND
IN A THOUSAND
SHADES OF
GREEN.

AND
WHEN
WE TURN AWAY ·
TO END THE DAY ·
FROM THE BRILLIANT
STAR · WE NEVER
SEE AT NIGHT · I WILL
LIE IN BED · AND
FILL MY HEAD · WITH
A MILLION SHADES
OF LIGHT.

CHERYL WHEELER

Gerry Jackson Kerdok

62

EMOTIONAL RESPONSE

New York summer night
Cabaret candlelight,
You walk in as I am speaking your name.
And moving over to where I stand
You squeeze when I take your hand.
I tell myself I've always been an emotional girl
but when I saw you walkin' in,
    I was taken once more
I don't know what for, it's just an

Emotional Response
Can't fight it, can't hide an emotional
  response
I'm walkin' the line - every time.

You don't have to be
Anything more to me,
I just want to see you once in a while.
I'm not looking to follow you
but somehow I always do.
I tell myself I'll play it cool till the feeling
  goes by.
I wonder who I think I'd fool
  with this look in my eye,
I don't even know why it's such an –

Emotional Response
Can't fight it, can't hide an emotional
  response
I'm walkin' the line - every time

And my heart beats fast, and I don't know why
And I tell myself I can take it all in stride.
I don't know if I can, I want control
I don't understand this emotional...

Emotional Response
Can't fight it, can't hide an emotional
  response
I'm walkin' the line - every time

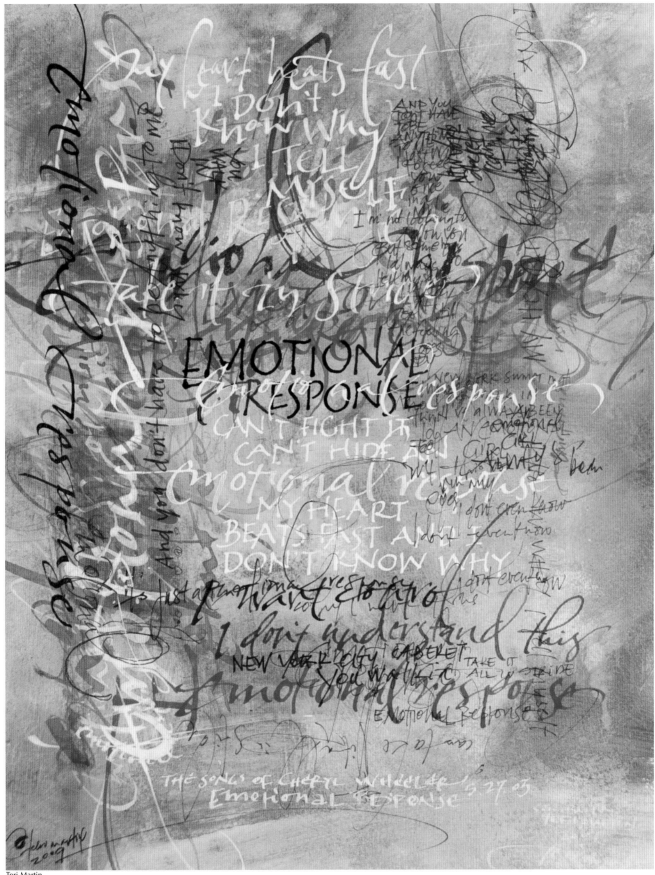

Teri Martin

IN YOUR HEART

You must have known when you
   caught my eye,
I've known it right from the start.
So tell me please; is there room for me
   in your heart?

I'll settle into dreamin' one more night,
Close my eyes and make it alright,
Dream about you, that's never gonna do it
   baby.
I'm walking these floors with a far away gaze,
Swear I'm gonna tell you one of these days.
But how would I try?
I'm strong until I look into your eyes.

How can it be when you talk to me,
You never see my desire?
How many times will I wake up
Feelin' on fire?

Every morning I try,
Tellin' myself it's a losin' game.
And everyday that goes by
I'm deeper in trouble
And breathing your name

IN YOUR HEART

Gwen Weaver

66

HOWL AT THE MOON

If I were maybe a wolf or a dog
I wouldn't have to speak
wouldn't have to talk
Just eat my dinner and go for a walk
And howl at the moon

And if I were laying there
just like you
All curled up the way dogs do
I'd dream that dream
that you're dreamin' too
And howl at the moon

And if I could carry
your black and white
Sleep so sound, wake so nice
I'd keep real close to my own advice
And howl at the moon

Oh, you know something I don't know
You go places I can't go
You lift your head
when the breezes blow
To voices older than time

I'll keep you close
Oh I like you near
I'll touch your head and pull your ear
And watch you resting while I sit here
And howl at the moon

YOU KNOW SOMETHING I DON'T KNOW
YOU GO PLACES I CAN'T GO
YOU LIFT YOUR HEAD WHEN THE BREEZES BLOW

TO VOICES OLDER THAN TIME
I'LL KEEP YOU CLOSE OH I LIKE YOU NEAR AND
WATCH YOU RESTING WHILE I SIT HERE
& HOWL AT THE MOON

Mary Lawler

BUT THE DAYS AND NIGHTS ARE LONG

Life is short, but the days and nights are long
Time will heal all these wounds
Someday soon, I'll be rising, I'll be strong
But now I'm losing all my battles
Now I'm down and dropping still
And this snow's blowing through
Like some ghost with this blue I know too well

Broken hearts keep on beating just the same
So I guess I can too, go through these moves
Facing forward, walking straight
But now my glance keeps drifting downward
Now my feet can't find their way
And this cold's creeping in
Through my bones, whisperin' it's here to stay

I'll bide my time - like there's any other way
It moves too slow, moves too fast
It's gone and passed and stopped entirely
 today
I know there's light on some horizon
But I can't see so far ahead
Patience and grace, blessed is love
I'm losin' my faith in most of that stuff
those wise men said
Most of that stuff those wise men said
Life is short, but the days and nights are long

Cherryl Moote

MOSQUITO

It's early in the season
to be suckin' my blood
musta just been this evenin'
you come up outta the mud
and I don't
mind I guess
you and your
proboscis
you can feast on me
first one's always free
I guess it must be
summertime

Mosquito

It's early in the season
to be suckin my blood
musta just been this evenin
you come up out of the mud
and I don't mind I guess
you and your
proboscis
you can feast on me
first one's always free
I guess it must be
summertime
Cheryl Wheeler

Ward Dunham

GANDHI/BUDDHA

Feel this wind blow
scatters all these leaves like paper rain
Feel these days roll
back into our winter lives again
The tangle at the garden fence is brown and dry
You call me out and point to your November sky

I must've been Gandhi or Buddha
or someone like that
I must've saved lives by the hundreds
everywhere I went
I must've brought rest to the restless
and fed the hungry too
I must've done something great
to get to have you

And when the cold comes
and you are by your fire and fast asleep
I'll turn a light on
to watch the snow outside fall soft and deep
And when the winter morning shines all white and blue
we'll watch the dogs run through the field like children do

I must've been Gandhi or Buddha
or someone like that
I must've saved lives by the hundreds
everywhere I went
I must've brought rest to the restless
and fed the hungry too
I must've done something great
to get to have you

And I suppose stranger things have come to pass
Many's the forest I can't see
I was so down and lost and fading fast
How did you find your way to me?

I must've been Gandhi or Buddha
or someone like that
I must've saved lives by the hundreds
everywhere I went
I must've brought rest to the restless
and fed the hungry too
I must've done something great
to get to have you

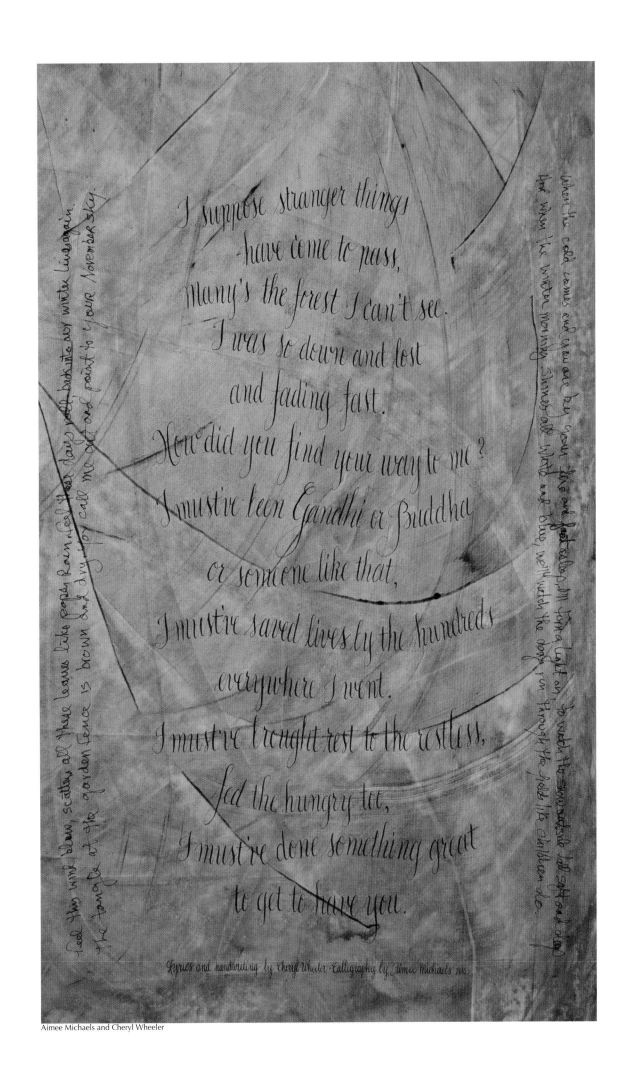

I suppose stranger things
have come to pass,
Many's the forest I can't see.
I was so down and lost
and fading fast.
How did you find your way to me?
I must've been Gandhi or Buddha
or someone like that,
I must've saved lives by the hundreds
everywhere I went.
I must've brought rest to the restless,
fed the hungry too,
I must've done something great
to get to have you.

Lyrics and handwriting by Cheryl Wheeler · Calligraphy by Aimee Michaels 2010

Aimee Michaels and Cheryl Wheeler

74

GANDHI/BUDDHA COUNTERVERSION

Man this wind blows, scatters all these leaves I've raked all day
And your snot nosed little cat keeps getting in the way
I've got to take that F-ing garden fence back down
Just so your local yokel friend can plow the ground

I must've been Hitler or Satan or someone like that
I must've caused death and destruction everywhere I went
I must've brought torts to the tortured, drowned some puppies too
I must've done something bad to have to have you

When the cold comes and you have turned the heat to 95
I'll put some shorts on, and wonder how the cats and dogs survive
And when the winter morning shines all white and blue
I'll tell you how it was when you get up at two

I must've been Hitler or Satan or someone like that
I must've caused death and destruction everywhere I went
I must've brought torts to the tortured, drowned some puppies too
I must've done something bad to have to have you

Listen, if stranger things have come to pass
Then they were in Rod Serling's head
I was just painting trim and sealing decks
Now I am stuck out here instead

I must've been Hitler or Satan or someone like that
I must've caused death and destruction everywhere I went
I must've brought torts to the tortured, drowned some puppies too
I must've done something bad to have to have you

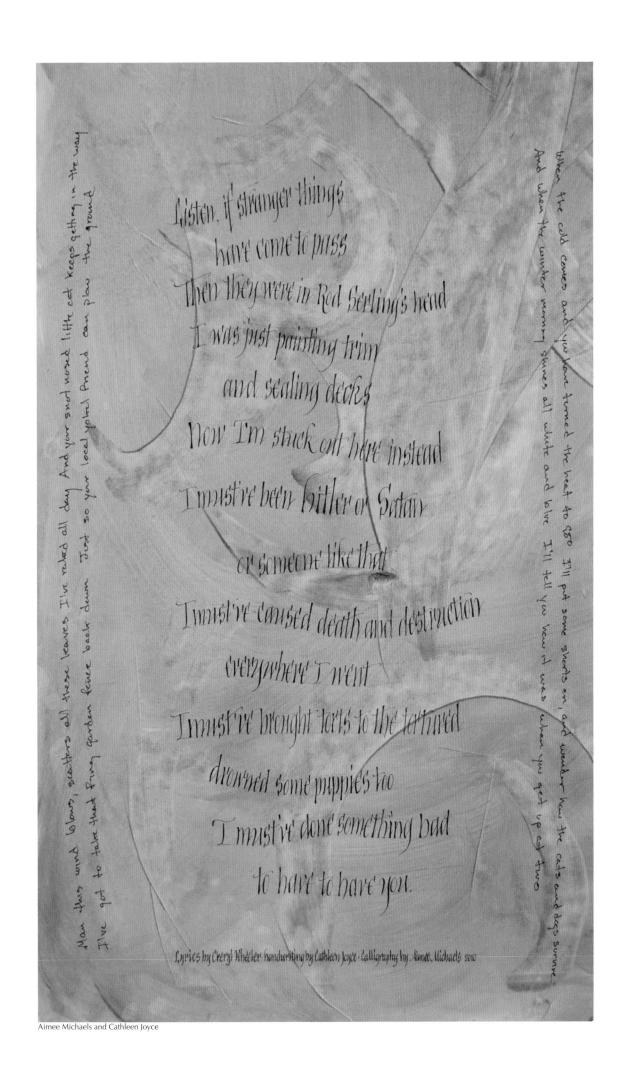

Listen, if stranger things
have come to pass
Then they were in Rod Serling's head
I was just painting trim
and sealing decks
Now I'm stuck out here instead
I must've been Hitler or Satan
or someone like that
I must've caused death and destruction
everywhere I went
I must've brought torts to the tortured
drowned some puppies too
I must've done something bad
to have to have you.

When the cold comes and you have turned the heat to 850 I'll put some shorts on, and wonder how the cats and dogs survive
And when the winter mummy shines all white and I die I'll tell you how it was when you got up at two

Man this wind blows, scatters all these leaves I've raked all day And your snot nosed little cat keeps getting in the way
I've got to take that friny garden fence back down Just so your local yokel friend can plow the ground

Lyrics by Cheryl Wheeler · handwriting by Cathleen Joyce · Calligraphy by Aimee Michaels 2010

Aimee Michaels and Cathleen Joyce

ROLLIN' BY

Here I go again
Another lonely song till the evenin' ends
Like a train rollin' around the bend
It's another lonely song rollin' by

One more rainy day
Streaky horizon, white and gray
Couldn't pour these clouds away
Heavy as night, deeper than blue

Here I go again
Another lonely song till the evenin' ends
Like a train rollin' around the bend
It's another lonely song rollin' by

Diesel train to carry me
Hear it approach, oh I can almost see
In my dreams I will always be
Goin' away travelin' home

Here I go again
Another lonely song till the evenin' ends
Like a train rollin' around the bend
It's another lonely song rollin' by

diesel train to
carry me
hear it approach
Oh I can almost see
in my dreams
I will always be

goin' away
travelin' home

CHERYL WHEELER

Pat Blair

ADDICTED

She says she hates to sleep alone, but she'll do it tonight
She wants to grab her telephone, but she knows it ain't right
So if he won't call she'll survive
And if he don't care she'll get by
Climb into bed, bury her head, and cry, cry
From the beginning he was all anyone could have been
They were delirious with love, they were certain to win
Now he's breaking plans more and more
And he's leaving notes on her door
'Took a trip out of town, couldn't turn this one down'
And 'I guess I should have told you before'

She says she feels like she's addicted to a real bad thing
Always sitting, waiting, wondering if the phone will ring
She knows she bounces like a yo-yo
   when he pulls her string
It hurts to feel like such a fool
She wants to tell him not to call or come around again
He doesn't need her now at all the way that she needs him
She's on the edge about to fall from leaning out and in
And she don't know which way to move

She wants to be fair, she couldn't say he was ever unkind
But if she could bear to walk away,
   she thinks he wouldn't mind
He just keeps himself so apart
And there's no one else in her heart
So she's taking a dive from an emotional high
And she's coming down hard
She's determined to try,
but she'll still give in when he gives her a call
She'll ask herself why, but in the end it won't matter at all
Sure she could sit at home, stay inside
And sleep alone with her pride
And as she walks out her door, she feels as weak as before
With nothing to hide

She says she feels like she's addicted to a real bad thing
Always sitting, waiting, wondering if the phone will ring
She knows she bounces like a yo-yo
   when he pulls her string
It hurts to feel like such a fool
She wants to tell him not to call or come around again
He doesn't need her now at all the way that she needs him
She's on the edge about to fall from leaning out and in
And she don't know which way to move

She says she hates to sleep alone, but she'll do it tonight. She wants to grab her telephone, but she knows it ain't right. So if he won't call she'll survive And if he don't care she'll get by Climb into bed bury her head and cry, cry. From the beginning he was all anyone could have been. They were delirious with love they were certain to win Now he's breaking plans more and more And he's leaving notes on her door 'took a trip out of town couldn't turn this one down' He said I guess I should have told you before' She says she feels like she's addicted to a real bad thing. She's always sitting waiting wondering if the phone will ring. She knows she bounces like a yo yo when he pulls her string It hurts to feel like such a fool. He wants to tell him not to call or come around again. He doesn't need her now at all the way that she needs him She's on the edge about to fall from leaning out and in And she don't know which way to move. She wants to be fair she couldn't say he was ever unkind. But if she could bear to walk away she thinks he wouldn't mind 'cause he just keeps himself so apart And there's no one else in her heart So she's taking a dive from an emotional high And coming down hard. She's determined to try but she'll still give in when he gives her a call. And she'll ask her self why but in the end it won't matter at all. Sure she could sit at home, stay inside And sleep alone with her pride And as she walks out her door, she feels as weak as before With nothing to hide. She says she feels like she's addicted to a real bad thing She's always sitting, waiting wondering if the phone will ring She knows she bounces like a yo-yo when he pulls her string It hurts to feel like such a fool. She wants to tell him not to call or come around again. He doesn't need her now at all the way that she needs him. She's on the edge about to fall from leaning out and in and she don't know which way to move. CHERYL WHEELER

CALLIGRAPHY & DESIGN: Jan Boyd

Jan Boyd

80

WHAT WE SAW

Oh darlin', I don't know how
I will make it through this night
I am lost and I am drifting way off course
And I need to lay my head down
in the cradle of your arms
See your face and feel your touch and hear your voice

In another situation I would surely rise above
And I'd stand apart and take a broader view
But I swear I wasn't watching
I did not expect this love
And I'm so surprised and so caught up in you

And we'll wear our hearts out
trying to do what's right
Feel our backs against the wall
And we'll turn our heads and
blink into this light
And if love is blind we won't know what we saw
Oh what we saw

There's a storm across the river
and a boat up on the sand
And a stone pile where a strong wall used to be
I was wading in this water when it dropped me where I am
With these waves and tides just washing over me

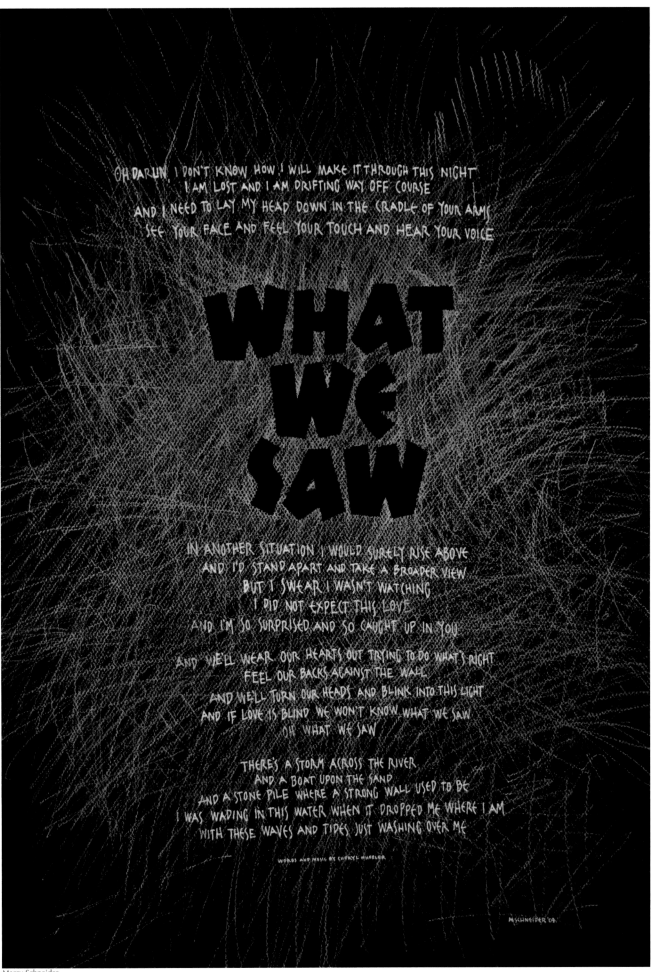

OH DARLIN, I DON'T KNOW HOW I WILL MAKE IT THROUGH THIS NIGHT
I AM LOST AND I AM DRIFTING WAY OFF COURSE
AND I NEED TO LAY MY HEAD DOWN IN THE CRADLE OF YOUR ARMS
SEE YOUR FACE AND FEEL YOUR TOUCH AND HEAR YOUR VOICE

WHAT WE SAW

IN ANOTHER SITUATION I WOULD SURELY RISE ABOVE
AND I'D STAND APART AND TAKE A BROADER VIEW
BUT I SWEAR I WASN'T WATCHING
I DID NOT EXPECT THIS LOVE
AND I'M SO SURPRISED AND SO CAUGHT UP IN YOU

AND WE'LL WEAR OUR HEARTS OUT TRYING TO DO WHAT'S RIGHT
FEEL OUR BACKS AGAINST THE WALL
AND WE'LL TURN OUR HEADS AND BLINK INTO THIS LIGHT
AND IF LOVE IS BLIND WE WON'T KNOW WHAT WE SAW
OH WHAT WE SAW

THERE'S A STORM ACROSS THE RIVER
AND A BOAT UPON THE SAND
AND A STONE PILE WHERE A STRONG WALL USED TO BE
I WAS WADING IN THIS WATER WHEN IT DROPPED ME WHERE I AM
WITH THESE WAVES AND TIDES JUST WASHING OVER ME

WORDS AND MUSIC BY CHERYL WHEELER

MSCHNEIDER '09

Marcy Schneider

PIPER

Early morning sunrise
come and pull the song from me,
So I can turn away
  and rest my tired eyes.
I can't escape the haunting
of a lonely melody,
It runs around and round
without a compromise.

So where you gonna go,
What you gonna do?
You know I can't say no,
Can't say good-bye to you.
I can't stop the flow
Till you've decided to.

The song runs like a piper,
like a drummer through my brain.
Silence all around
feels so apart from me.
And I could sit and cry
for all the love and all the pain,
That brings itself to mind
inside a harmony.

The softest mornin' light
Can't shine as soft as you.
The sweetest love in sight
Can't love me like you do.
The swiftest bird in flight
Can't climb the path to you.

Now it's fully dawn
and nightly silence breaks away,
Into the distant sounds
of cars and factories.
Traces linger on
and slowly fade into the day,
And leave me with these rounds
all hummin' back to me.
So now I bid you well
and take myself to bed.
The tune you had to tell
was soft and kindly said,
And I still feel the swell
from all you comforted.

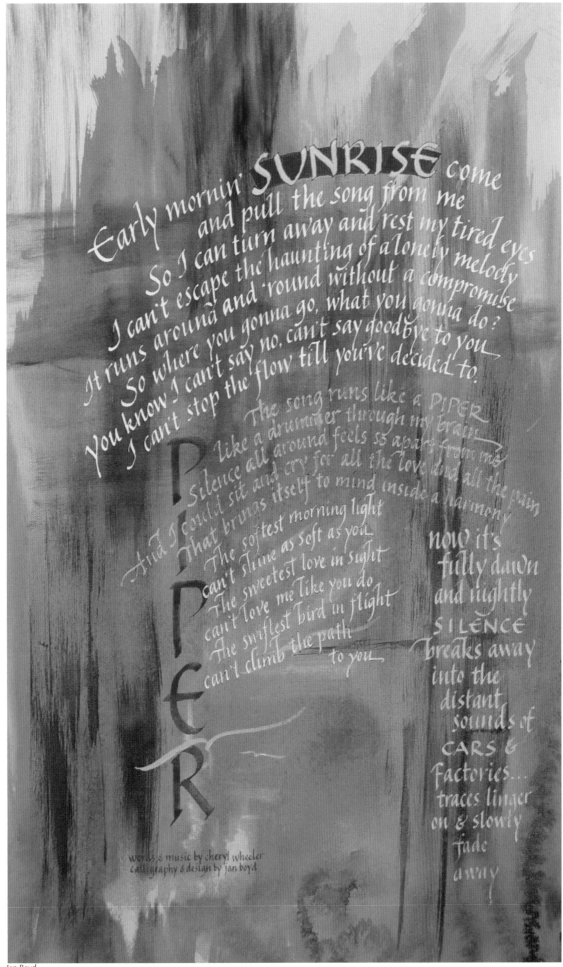

Early mornin' SUNRISE come
and pull the song from me
So I can turn away and rest my tired eyes
I can't escape the haunting of a lonely melody
It runs around and 'round without a compromise
So where you gonna go, what you gonna do?
You know I can't say no, can't say goodbye to you
I can't stop the flow till you've decided to.

The song runs like a PIPER
Like a drummer through my brain
Silence all around feels so apart from me
And I could sit and cry for all the love and all the pain
That brings itself to mind inside a harmony
The softest morning light
can't shine as soft as you
The sweetest love in sight
can't love me like you do
The swiftest bird in flight
can't climb the path
to you,

PIPER

now it's
fully dawn
and nightly
SILENCE
breaks away
into the
distant
sounds of
CARS &
Factories...
traces linger
on & slowly
fade
away

words & music by cheryl wheeler
calligraphy & design by jan boyd

Jan Boyd

84

MY CAT'S BIRTHDAY

On my cat's birthday the mice did sway
And the squirrels did dance around
The dogs went nuts when they heard such fuss,
And hustled out to party down
The little birds tap-danced all around the ants
Moving in a conga line
Weasel band played, lady bugs made
  crocus and azalea wine
Sitting at the tables in their pirate blouses
Guess they got the furniture from outta their houses
Out back at the volleyball,
 toads had to argue every call
Crows showed up in the cop outfits,
  holsters sliding off their hips
Deer hung back by the garden shed,
  turkeys scratched in the flowerbed

On my cat's birthday the birthday cake
  was several stories high
Cats ate down along the ground, birds ate in the sky
And the squirrels ate too from the edge of the roof
Till they finally jumped right in
But the band played on till the cake was gone
We'll never see another again

Catnip came and it all went south.
Where did that goldfinch get that mouth?
Dogs growling over bones they'd buried,
A rabbit and a robin got married.
Band started singing 'bout a love so deep
Guest of honor drifted off to sleep
Curled around another old cat dream
And that's how Penrod turned 15

On my cat's
BIRTHDAY
the mice
did
sway
the squirrels did
DANCE
DOGS went
NUTS
the little bird tap danced
A weasel BAND played
ALL AROUND THE
Ants
made crocus and azalea WINE
TOADS had to argue
CROWS showed UP
DEER hung back
TURKEYS scratched
the BIRTHDAY CAKE was several stories HIGH
CATS ate!
BIRDS ate.
SQUIRRELS ate.
The guest of honor
DRIFTED off to SLEEP.
The BAND played.
PENROD
turned
15

Amy Veaner

86

UNWORTHY

I'm unworthy - and no matter what I'm doing
I should certainly be doing something else
And it's selfish, to be thinking I'm unworthy
All this me me me me self self self self self
If I'm talking on the phone I should be working on the lawn
which looks disgraceful from the things I haven't done
If I'm working on the lawn I should be concentrating on
those magazines inside, since I have not read one

I should learn how to meditate and sew and bake
and dance and paint and sail and make gazpacho
I should turn my attention to repairing
all those forty year old socks there in that bureau
I should let someone teach me to run Windows
and learn French that I can read and write and speak.
I should get life in prison for how I treated my parents
from third grade until last week

And I should spend more time playing with my dog
and much less money on this needless junk I buy
I should send correspondence back to everyone
who's written, phoned or faxed since Jr. High
I should sit with a therapist until I understand
the way I felt back in my mom
I should quit smoking, drinking, eating, thinking
sleeping, watching TV, writing stupid songs

And I should be less impatient when the line just takes forever
'cause the two cashiers are talking
I should see what it's like to get up really early, rain or shine,
and spend three hours walking
I should know CPR and deep massage and Braille
and Sign Language and how to change my oil
I should go where the situation's desperate
and build and paint and trudge and tote and toil

And I should chant in impossible positions
till my legs appear to not have any bones
I should rant at the cops and politicians
and the corporations in indignant tones
I should save lots of money to leave Audubon
plus all the rocks and animals and plants
I should brave possibilities for plotting plums of problems
probably blossomed, plausibly from
blah blah blah blah blah blah blah blah
blah blah blah blah blah blah blah blah
I'm unworthy

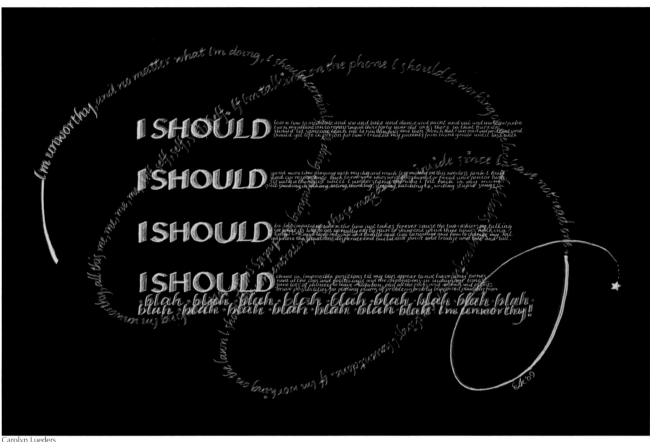

Carolyn Lueders

SOON AS I FIND MY VOICE

Soon as I find my voice - talk to you all night
Soon as I get these words - get these words just right
Soon as I think I see you - clearly in my sight
Soon as I find my - soon as I find my voice

Soon as I see my road - walk the straightest line
Soon as I know what's yours - understand what's mine
Soon as I hear in sync I'll be, singing all the time
Soon as I find my, soon as I find my voice

There seems to be, something whispering to me
I don't hear a thing - all night
Something been blowin' around outside
Something been draggin' me down

Soon as I learn these ropes - bound to win this fight
Soon as I know what's wrong - try to do what's right
Soon as I get this darkness –closer to the light
Soon as I find my - soon as I find my voice

Soon as I hit my stride - run the course on time
Soon as I catch your light - do my best to shine
Soon as I know my part - I'll be practicing my lines
Soon as I find my - soon as I find my voice

Soon as I see ✦ **Soon as I know** ✦ find · get · think · see · know · hear · learn · hit · catch · Soon as I hear ✦ **Soon as I learn** ✦ Soon as I hit ✦ **Soon as I find** ✦ Soon soon ✦ Soon oh, so soon as I find my ✦ Soon as I get ✦ **Soon as I catch** ✦ **Soon as I think** ✦

Soon as I find my voice
— Cheryl Wheeler —
— Norma McKenzie

Norma McKenzie

CAT ACCOUNTANT

My cat accountant taps his furry head
His visor's green and all my numbers are red
His little lamp is burning all the time
  and what is his used to be mine

His calculating is so round about
Einstein and Hawking couldn't figure it out
Bill Gates and Midas wouldn't make a dime
  with my CPA feline

If you saw him on the street you'd never guess
What those pencils in his pocket sleeve are for
He may look soft and sweet but now hear this
He's a ruthless little cat entrepreneur
Bottom line and business to the core

He zips through my room in his racing car
He dips his beetles into caviar
He has his snowboards jetted in from France
And he busts a sag in baggy black leather pants

If you're staying in a really nice hotel
And a white cat takes the table next to you
You will find his dining charges on your bill
With his room and tax and transportation too
And there will not be a thing that you can do

He is a Tiger at the driving range
He keeps a locker at the stock exchange
Even his cell phone has a diamond ring
  and all day long I hear it sing
Cha-ching cha-ching
Cha-ching cha-ching
Cha-ching cha-ching
Cha-ching

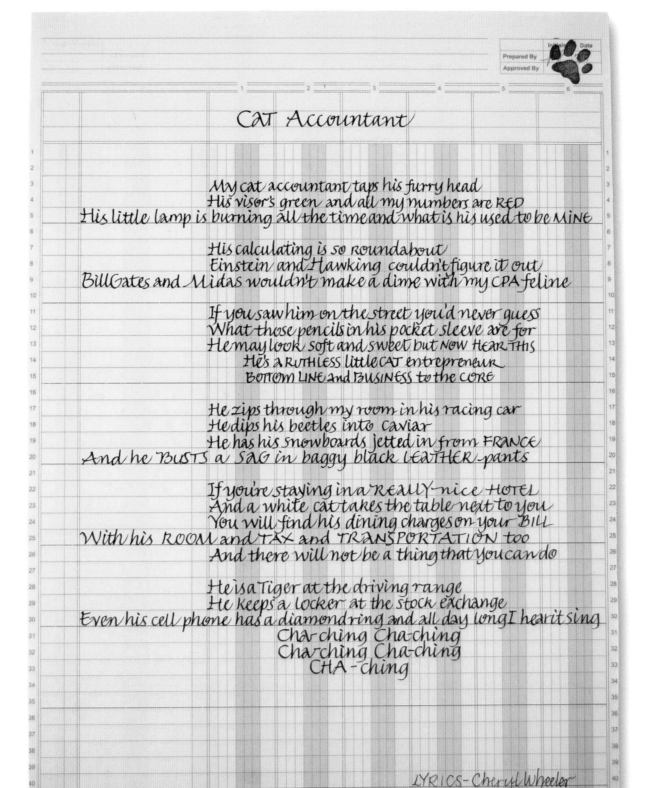

CAT Accountant

My cat accountant taps his furry head
His visor's green and all my numbers are RED
His little lamp is burning all the time and what is his used to be MINE

His calculating is so roundabout
Einstein and Hawking couldn't figure it out
Bill Gates and Midas wouldn't make a dime with my CPA feline

If you saw him on the street you'd never guess
What those pencils in his pocket sleeve are for
He may look soft and sweet but NOW HEAR THIS
He's a RUTHLESS little CAT entrepreneur
BOTTOM LINE and BUSINESS to the CORE

He zips through my room in his racing car
He dips his beetles into caviar
He has his snowboards jetted in from FRANCE
And he BUSTS a SAG in baggy black LEATHER pants

If you're staying in a REALLY nice HOTEL
And a white cat takes the table next to you
You will find his dining charges on your BILL
With his ROOM and TAX and TRANSPORTATION too
And there will not be a thing that you can do

He is a Tiger at the driving range
He keeps a locker at the stock exchange
Even his cell phone has a diamond ring and all day long I hear it sing
Cha-ching Cha-ching
Cha-ching Cha-ching
CHA-ching

LYRICS - Cheryl Wheeler
Lettering - Patte Leathe

Patte Leathe

WHEN FALL COMES TO NEW ENGLAND

When fall comes to New England
The sun slants in so fine
And the air's so clear
You can almost hear the grapes grow on the vine

The nights are sharp with starlight
The days are cool and clean
And in the blue sky overhead
The northern geese fly south instead
And leaves are Irish Setter red
When fall comes to New England

When fall comes to New England
And the wind blows off the sea
Swallows fly in a perfect sky
And the world was meant to be

When the acorns line the walkways
Then winter can't be far
From yellow leaves a blue jay calls
Grandmothers walk out in their shawls
And chipmunks run the old stone walls
When fall comes to New England

The frost is on the pumpkin
The squash is off the vine
And winter warnings race across the sky
The squirrels are on to something
And they're working overtime
The foxes blink and stare and so do I

'Cause when fall comes to New England
Oh I can't turn away
From fading light on flying wings
And late goodbyes a robin sings
And then another thousand things
When fall comes to New England

the nights are sharp with starlight
and the days are cool and clean
and in the blue sky overhead
the northern geese fly south instead
and leaves are irish setter red
when fall comes to new england

when fall comes to new england
and the wind blows off the sea
swallows fly in a perfect sky
and the world was meant to be

when the acorns line the walkways
then winter can't be far
from yellow leaves a blue jay calls
grandmothers walk out in their shawl
and chipmunks run the old stone walls
when fall comes to new england

Alesia Zorn

94

PRAISE THE LORD AND LIFE IS GRAND

Praise the lord and life is grand and man I feel so crazy
Quite a leap from who I am, to who I want to be
I woke up this morning with the heaviest of hearts
Don't know where the blue sky ends
    and where the gray one starts

I don't need no comforting,
    no pills to make me happy
Little pills to take until I just can't feel a thing
I can drone these words until they haunt me
    like a ghost
They can be the medicine that touches me the most

All the day the clouds will lay
    the winter gray above me
And all the night, the snowy sight,
    the glowing light so lovely

I can't make this go away,
    can't shake this from my shoulders
I can be so slow to see what everyone has seen
Wish I didn't feel this way but I'm afraid I do
Wish I had ten thousand stars to offer up to you

Praise the lord and life is grand and man I feel so crazy

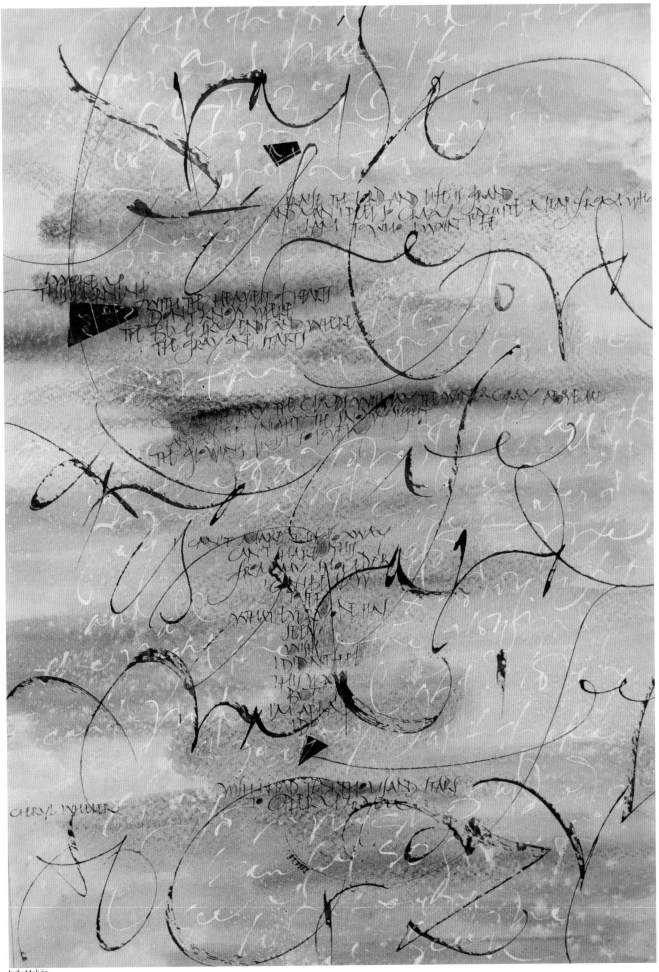

Judy Melvin

HERE COME FLOYD

Here come Floyd, tally-ho
Out he come, in we go
Dark, dark, dark
Blow, blow, blow
Rain, rain, rain, rain, rain
Florida to Maine

Weather channel satellite
  keep us well informed all night
Like CNN, ABC
  and every station on TV

'Cause it's a big one, Lord yes
It's a big one, I guess
And we are deep in trouble
When all the trees bend double

Howlin' wind, scary sound
Everythin' blow around
Pacing dogs wonder if
We have even noticed this

Do you want to? Well alright,
  but if we do we'll munch all night
Put pillows in your comfy chair
And hope the outside stays out there

'Cause it's a big one, Lord yes
It's a big one, I guess
And we are deep in trouble
When all the trees bend double

Here come Floyd, tally-ho
Out he come, in we go
Dark, dark, dark
Blow, blow, blow
Rain, rain, rain, rain, rain
Florida to Maine

Adam Heller and Tracy Mahaffey

IF IT WERE UP TO ME

Maybe it's the movies, maybe it's the books
Maybe it's the bullets, maybe it's the real crooks
Maybe it's the drugs, maybe it's the parents
Maybe it's the colors everybody's wearin'
Maybe it's the President, maybe it's the last one
Maybe it's the one before that, what he done
Maybe it's the high schools, maybe it's the teachers
Maybe it's the tattooed children in the bleachers
Maybe it's the Bible, maybe it's the lack
Maybe it's the music, maybe it's the crack
Maybe it's the hairdos, maybe it's the TV
Maybe it's the cigarettes, maybe it's the family
Maybe it's the fast food, maybe it's the news
Maybe it's divorce, maybe it's abuse
Maybe it's the lawyers, maybe it's the prisons
Maybe it's the Senators, maybe it's the system
Maybe it's the fathers, maybe it's the sons
Maybe it's the sisters, maybe it's the moms
Maybe it's the radio, maybe it's road rage
Maybe El Nino, or UV rays
Maybe it's the army, maybe it's the liquor
Maybe it's the papers, maybe the militia
Maybe it's the athletes, maybe it's the ads
Maybe it's the sports fans, maybe it's a fad
Maybe it's the magazines, maybe it's the internet
Maybe it's the lottery, maybe it's the immigrants
Maybe it's taxes, big business
Maybe it's the KKK and the skinheads
Maybe it's the communists, maybe it's the Catholics
Maybe it's the hippies, maybe it's the addicts
Maybe it's the art, maybe it's the sex
Maybe it's the homeless, maybe it's the banks
Maybe it's the clearcut, maybe it's the ozone
Maybe it's the chemicals, maybe it's the car phone
Maybe it's the fertilizer, maybe it's the nose rings
Maybe it's the end, but I know one thing.
If it were up to me, I'd take away the guns.

Maybe it's the addicts
Maybe it's the banks
Maybe it's the homeless
Maybe it's the lawyers
M Maybe it's the communist
Maybe it's the sea
Maybe it's the art
Maybe it's the catholics

Maybe it's the family
Maybe it's the cigarettes
Maybe it's the hairdos
M Maybe it's the Bible
Maybe it's the crack
Maybe it's the music

Maybe it's the chemical, Maybe it's the car phones, Maybe it's the fertilizer, Maybe it's the nose rings

Maybe it's the end but I know one thing...

If it were up to me I'd take away the Guns
Cheryl Wheeler

Angel Huertas

THIS IS ME

Somedays I can tell
You are holding back the river with a broken dam
And sometimes do you feel
  like you're riding with the wrong reins in your hand?
Don't tell yourself you have used up all your chances
This is me talkin' now
This is me who loves you still
And you know I always will

Some things never change
You were always just the one I couldn't live without
I can't turn some page
And pretend it's all undone and I don't love you now
You close your eyes, and remember what I told you
This is me talkin' now
This is me who loves you still
And you know I always will

So let it go little darlin'
Go on back to sleep
There are no bridges burnin'
Between you and me

We have years to fill
Yes and all the days behind us for believin' in
And we have tales to tell
And we would always have Paris if we'd ever been
I feel your heart, beating true across this distance
This is me talkin' now
This is me who loves you still
And you know I always will

Close your eyes
and remember
what I told you
This is me talkin now
This is me
who loves you still
and you know
I always will

~ Cheryl Wheeler ~

Harvest Crittenden

102

NORTHERN GIRL

Why are the rain clouds comin', pourin' down on me?
Why can't the north wind turn and blow the other way?
Where has the sunshine gone? Oh I can barely see,
This northern rain is fallin', and home is callin' me.
Sun in a southern sky is all I need to see.
Just watchin' a small bird fly, above the fields and me
Walkin' a dusty road and there's nothin' 'round the bend
except those golden tones of goin' home again.

Goin' home - goin' home

Muddy old river flowin' neath a fallen tree,
Sunflower garden growin' twice as tall as me
Sister and father hear me, what I've learned today
I ain't no northern girl, I've been too long away.

Goin' home - goin' home

On a starry old summer evenin' hummin' warm and sweet
I hit the road believin' I was bound to leave
It took a New England sky to teach me how to say
I ain't no northern girl, I've been too long away
I ain't no northern girl, I've been too long away

This ain't no northern song - I've been too long away.

why are the rain clouds comin' pourin' down on me?
why cant the north wind turn and blow the other way?
WHERE HAS the SUNSHINE GONE?
Oh I can barely see
this northern rain
is fallin' and home
is callin' me

SUN IN A SOUTHERN SKY
IS ALL I NEED TO SEE
WATCHIN' A SMALL BIRD FLY
ABOVE THE FIELDS AND ME
WALKIN' A DUSTY ROAD
AND THERE'S SO THIN
'ROUND THE BEND
EXCEPT THOSE GOLDEN TONES
OF GOIN' HOME AGAIN

goin' home goin' home

MUDDY OLD RIVER FLOWIN'
'NEATH A FALLEN TREE

On a starry old   everything
summer evening   garden growin'
hummin' warm   twice as
and sweet   tall
                                    as me
SISTER AND FATHER
HEAR ME WHAT I'VE
LEARNED TODAY
I hit the road believin'   I AINT NO NORTHERN
I was bound to leave   I've been too GIRL
                              long away

goin' home goin' home

IT TOOK
a new england sky to teach me how to say
I aint no northern girl I've been too long away
I ain't no northern girl, I've been too long away
This aint no northern song
I've been too long away.

LYRICS BY CHERYL WHEELER
Art and Calligraphy by Connie Furgason

Connie Furgason

BLESSED

Dancing in our rooms, you knew all the moves
Thinkin' of Mom in saddle shoes, it was amazing
Laughing family, long Monopoly
Sunday night TV, Adam and Hop Sing

We were as blessed as blessed can be
You and Mom and Dad and me
Singin' in 4 part harmony
"I Love To Tell The Story"

Me and my guitar, softball in the yard
Breezeway playin' cards with half of the neighborhood
Their crazy bridge club nights, Sunday back road drives
Running for our lives down into Rhode's woods

We were as blessed as blessed can be
You and Mom and Dad and me
Singin' in 4 part harmony
"I Love To Tell The Story"

And it seemed like something just this side of heaven
Comin' from the AM radio
And it felt like it would just go on forever
Singin "Long Time Man" and "Pretty Peggy-o"

Now we're old and gray, mem'ries fade away
These are here to stay, that is our blessing

We were as blessed as blessed can be
You and Mom and Dad and me
Singin' in 4 part harmony
"I Love To Tell The Story"

"I love to tell the story
'Twill be my theme in glory
To tell the old, old story
Of Jesus and his love"

"I love to tell the story" is an old hymn written by:
Katherine Hankey ca 1868 – Lyrics
William G. Fischer 1869 - Music

Blessed

Cheryl Wheeler

Dancing in our rooms, you knew all the moves
Thinkin' of Mom in saddle shoes
It was amazing
Laughing family, long Monopoly
Sunday night TV, Adam and Hoss Sing

We were as blessed as blessed can be
You and Mom and Dad and me
Singin' in four part harmony
"I Love To Tell The Story"

Me and my guitar, softball in the yard
Breezeway playin' cards with half of the neighborhood
Their crazy bridge club nights, Sunday back road drives
Running for our lives down into Rhodes woods

And it seemed like something just this side of heaven
Comin' from the AM radio
And it felt like it would just go on forever
Singin' "Long Time Man" and "Pretty Peggy-o"

Now we're old and gray, mem'ries fade away
These are here to stay, that is our blessing

Ruth Korch

I LOVE TO TELL THE STORY TWILL BE MY THEME IN GLORY TO TELL THE OLD OLD STORY OF JESUS AND HIS LOVE

LITTLE ROAD

How can there be trouble in this world?
With the color in these hills, the blue October sky,
  this little road that winds along the river
Dusty barns and tractors in the fields
And families sit in front yards, or stand outside the churches
Kids are throwing footballs and pulling carts of pumpkins
And the morning sun is sparkling on the water

How can there be such trouble in this world?
Where the mountains roll so gently,
  deer graze on the hillsides, birds chat on the phone lines
The whole wide world's a prayer for Sunday morning
The geese inspect the stubble in the fields
And all along the roadside, families stop to wonder
At the new October morning
And a red tailed hawk is circling
And a father hugs his daughter
And an old man holds the car door for his wife to come and see
Then they turn and smile at me.
How can there be such trouble in this world

I know, of course I know, that this is not the only picture
I don't, of course I don't, know what to do

But the road keeps winding through the afternoon
And it doesn't know the sorrow, or an inkling of the shadow
  of the rage across the water, the hatred and the horror.
It just wanders through this valley with the river by its side
As the light fades from the sky
The beautiful light fades from the sky

Sharon Zeugin

WHO AM I FOOLIN'?

I can go through the motions, sometimes I swear I'm okay
Sure I miss you, but I've been really movin', really turnin' away.
But just when I thought the heartache was gone
It's tapping me on the shoulder
Sayin' who are you foolin', some things you just don't get over

I could write you a letter, and I always do in my head
Just to tell you I'm better and this lonely didn't kill me I guess
But just when I know I've finally let go
I dream you are so much closer
Oh who am I foolin', some things you just don't get over

I'm wearin' a new face, a little insane
And here in the old place nothing's the same

I'm waiting for winter, it always seems warmer somehow
It's the sun on the snowfall and the silence I am longing for now
But with one backward glance, I won't stand a chance
So I'll wave goodbye over my shoulder
Oh who am I foolin', some things you just don't get over

Always seems warmer somehow. It's the sun
falling on the snow I'll wave goodbye over my shoulder. Yeah who
21:43 LATER since, so I'll wave goodbye over my shoulder.

I'm waiting for winter...
one backward glance, I won't stand a
chance, I won't get over...
with one backward glance, I just don't get over...
silence I am longing for now, but some things you just don't
silence I am longing for now, and I foolin'
the who am I foolin'?

WHO AM I FOOLIN?

Words & Music
Cheryl Wheeler

Artwork
Amy Pfleiger 2010

Amy Pfleiger

110

ESTATE SALE

Estate sale - today from one o'clock to four
You go and get ready, I'll go start the car
Better to be early, then we'll be the first in line
You know how I love this, it's amazing what you'll find

Going through dead peoples houses
Wonderful things they have collected
Open the drawers and trunks and closets
Don't leave a corner uninspected

I'll head for the kitchen - you check out upstairs
Old postcards 'n' pens 'n' blue fiesta wear
Shaving mugs 'n' winged eyeglasses - giant plastic pins
Linen suits and flowered dresses - I'm so glad we got in

Going through dead peoples houses
Wonderful things they have collected
Open the drawers and trunks and closets
Don't leave a corner uninspected

They just don't make 'em like this
It's an incredible prize
We can hang it in the kitchen
She was just your size
It's a beautiful frame
And the picture's alright
Salt and pepper airplanes
And that deco light

Going through dead peoples houses
Wonderful things they have collected
Open the drawers and trunks and closets
Don't leave a corner uninspected

Tonight we'll go home and sort through our array
We'll find the best spots to put things on display
You can't get this great stuff anymore, I don't know why
But I bet we'll make some young strangers
Happy when we die

Going through dead peoples houses
Wonderful things they have collected
Open the drawers and trunks and closets
Don't leave a corner uninspected

ESTATE SALE TODAY, FROM 1 o'clock TO 4
YOU GO GET READY, I'LL GO START THE CAR
BETTER TO BE EARLY, THEN WE'LL BE THE
FIRST IN LINE. AND YOU KNOW HOW I LOVE THIS.
IT'S AMAZING WHAT YOU'LL FIND,
going through dead people's houses
I'LL HEAD FOR THE KITCHEN YOU CHECK OUT UPSTAIRS
OLD POSTCARDS AND PENS AND BLUE FIESTA WARE
SHAVING MUGS AND WINGED/eye GLASSES
GIANT PLASTIC PINS, LINEN SUITS AND
FLOWERED DRESSES, I'M SO GLAD WE GOT IN
Wonderful things they have collected
THEY JUST DON'T MAKE 'EM LIKE THIS
IT'S AN INCREDIBLE PRIZE
WE CAN HANG IT IN THE KITCHEN
SHE WAS JUST YOUR SIZE
IT'S A BEAUTIFUL FRAME
AND THE PICTURE'S ALL RIGHT
SALT AND PEPPER AIRPLANES
AND THAT DECO LIGHT
Open the drawers and trunks and closets
TONIGHT WE'LL GO HOME AND
SORT THROUGH OUR ARRAY
WE'LL FIND THE BEST SPOTS
TO PUT THINGS ON DISPLAY
YOU CAN'T GET THIS GREAT STUFF ANYMORE
I DON'T KNOW WHY
BUT I BET WE'LL MAKE SOME
YOUNG STRANGERS
HAPPY WHEN WE DIE
Don't leave a corner uninspected

ESTATE SALE · the songs of Cheryl Wheeler
5·18·1988
Teri Martin 2009

Teri Martin

112

SUMMER FLY

In another, younger day I could dream the time away
In the universe inside my room
And the world was really mine from June to September
And if it wasn't really so, I was lucky not to know
And I was lucky not to wonder why
'cause a starry sky is all that I remember

A summer fly was buzzin'
   every night when I was young
In the gentle world my child-like senses knew
And the world was just my cousin
   and the wind was just the tongue
In the voice my lonely moments listened to

And I look at me today, all the dreams have gone away
And I'm where I never thought I'd be
Seeing things I never thought I'd see happening to me
And I lay awake at night, till the darkness goes to light
Hearing voices calling out my name
Droning over and again the same message through me

Cryin' who's your partner, who's your darlin'
   who's your baby now?
Who wakes up at night to pull you in?
It don't matter, you just make her lonely anyhow
Don't know why you even try to win

Oh this'll never fly, get out while you can
Look into the mirror say it's not the same again
Every single time, things just fall apart
Slamming door, slipping pride, sad and angry heart

Who's your partner, who's your darlin'
   who's your baby now?
Who wakes up at night to pull you in?
It don't matter, you just make her lonely anyhow
Don't know why you even try to win

In another, younger day I could dream the time away
In the universe inside my room
And the world was really mine from June to September

the starry sky is all that I remember

And I look at me today And I look at me today
all the dreams have gone away all the dreams have gone away
And I'm where I never thought I'd be
Seeing things I never thought I'd see happen to me
And I lay awake at night 'till the darkness
goes to light Hearin' voices callin' out my name
DRONIN' OVER AND AGAIN over and again
the same message to me CRYIN'
WHO'S YOUR PARTNER, WHO'S YOUR DARLIN'
WHO'S YOUR BABY NOW? who wakes up at
night to pull you in? It don't matter you just
make her lonely anyhow. Don't know why you
even try to win Oh, this'll never fly, get out
while you can LOOK INTO THE
MIRROR say it's not the
same again
Every single time things just fall apart
SLAMMING DOOR
SLIPPING PRIDE Sad and
ANGRY
HEART
Crying who's your partner,
who's your darlin' who's your
baby now? Who wakes up at night
to pull you in? It don't matter
you just make her lonely anyhow
Don't know why you even try
Don't know why to win
Don't know why

In another younger day I could dream the time away
In the universe inside my room
AND THE WORLD WAS REALLY MINE
from june to september And if it wasn't really so
I was lucky not to know And I was lucky not to wonder why
'Cause the starry sky is all that I remember
the starry sky is all that I remember
A summer fly was buzzin' every night when I was young
the gentle world my childlike senses knew
And the world was just my cousins And the world
was just the tongue In the voice my lonely moments listened to

Summer Fly Words by Cheryl Wheeler
Calligraphy by Carol Percy 2009

Carol Percy

114

SYLVIA HOTEL

This is a lonely life
As I know you know too well
I'm thinking of you tonight,
Here in the Sylvia Hotel

Smoking a cigarette
Drinking a glass of beer
Catching a conversation
I am trying not to hear

One more
Why not, okay
Guess I'm glad I came
To stare at English Bay
Under all the rain

There's a cat in this bar right now
Twitching his tail away
I called with a soft meow
Maybe he only speaks Francais

You must be safe in bed
Down in your cowboy home
I don't wonder why you left
I wonder why you stayed so long

One more
Why not, okay
I'm glad I came
And here's to English Bay
In the lovely rain

Found some matches from Durango
In my pocket
But if I let my heart get sad
Then I can't stop it

And this is a lonely life
Though I think it suits me well
And everything's fine tonight
Here in the Sylvia Hotel

AND THIS IS A
LONELY
LIFE
THOUGH I THINK
IT SUITS ME WELL
AND EVERYTHING'S
FINE TONIGHT
HERE IN THE
SYLVIA HOTEL

Bev Allen and Erin Allen

116

MUSIC IN MY ROOM

In my secret hideaway, I would play all night
So if you go out, hope you don't want me to
I've got a rendezvous with a stack of 45s

Saturday night, sittin' home alone
Disconnect the phone - put those records on
Up in my room, tryin' to find the chords
Learning all the words to all my favorite songs
I love to hear those voices talk in rhyme
I know I've played this one a hundred times
And I know the songs will end too soon
When I'm listening to the music in my room

Up in my bed, by the radio
Kept it turned so low - listening in the dark
Closing my eyes, whispering along
Waiting for the song that always hit the mark
I counted twos and fours instead of sheep
I sailed across the Mersey in my sleep
And I knew the songs would end too soon
When I listened to the music in my room

And it was something to keep with me where I went
Secret and seductive in my ear
Wondering at all those hours spent
Lost in something I could only hear

Saturday night, always here and gone
Sunday comes along - Friday seems so far
Sitting in school, groovin' in my chair
Tap the desk and stare, dream of my guitar
I drifted off in waves of rock and roll
I wondered if I had a rubber soul
And I knew the songs would end too soon
When I listened to the music in my room

So if you go out, hope you don't want me to
I've got a rendezvous with a stack of 45s

Music in My Room

In my secret hideaway, I would play all night
So if you go out, hope you don't want me to.
I've got a rendezvous with a stack of forty fives
Saturday night sittin' home alone disconnect the phone
Put these records on.
Up in my room, tryin' to find the chords learning all the words
To all my favorite songs.
I love to hear those voices talk in rhymes
I know I've played this one a hundred times
And I know the songs will end too soon,
When I'm listenin' to the music in my room
In my bed by the radio
Kept it turned so low listnin' in the dark
Closing my eyes, whispering along
Waiting for the song that always hit the mark
I counted two's and four's instead of sheep
I sailed across the Mersey in my sleep
And I knew the songs would end too soon
When I listened to the music in my room
It was something to take with me where I went
Secret and seductive in my ear
Oh, wondering if all those hours spent
Lost in something I could only hear
Saturday night always here and gone
Sunday comes along
Friday seems so far
Sitting in school, groovin' in my chair
Tap the desk and stare
And dream of my guitar
I drifted off in waves of rock and roll
And I wondered if "I had a rubber soul"
And I knew the songs would end too soon
When I listened to the music in my room
So if you go out hope you don't want me to
I've got a rendezvous with a stack of forty fives.

Words and music by Cheryl Wheeler

Mike Kecseg

THE STORM

Trouble on the rise
from the middle of a stormy sea
Muffled in the skies
on the edges of the whole country
Blowing home heavy hearts again
In a moan, frozen on the wind
I never knew a sky so grey
On an icy day
As the wind blows down
On a sea coast town

Harboring the beast
that the power of the wind controls
Howling in the streets
with the voices of the ancient souls
Old and frail primeval mysteries
Come to wail of unknown histories
And I never heard a stronger cry
From a mournful sky
Over frozen land
In the winter's hand

Out along the shore
in a hurricane of ice and foam
Swaying in the roar
I was standing on the dock alone
In the night
Where the forces came to play
And maybe I
Should have known to turn away
But I never felt so drawn and bound
To the great unknown
Till it turned me around
And it sent me home

Trouble on the rise from
the middle of a stormy sea
Muffled in the skies on the edges
of the whole country
Blowing home
heavy hearts again
In a moan, frozen on the wind
I never knew a sky so gray
On an icy day as the wind
blows down on a seacoast town.

Harboring the beast that the power
of the wind controls, Howling in the
streets with the voices of the ancient souls
Old and frail primeval mysteries
I never heard a stronger cry
from a mournful sky
over frozen land in the winter's hand
Out along the shore in a hurricane of ice
and foam, Swaying in the roar I was standing
on the dock alone in the night where the
forces came to play and maybe I should have
known to turn away. But I never felt so drawn
and bound to the great unknown til it turned
me around and sent me home.

Roann Mathias

120

ACT OF NATURE

The wind came round and blew this place apart
It's you and me now sitting in the dark
The lights are out and everybody's home
It's you and me and we are both alone

The lines are down there's just no getting through
You stare at me and I stare back at you
And in the dark I know that I can't see
'Cause here you are and still you don't see me

Act of nature, act of God
Raging through our sedentary lives
We are on the brink
We are floundering
Spinning in this dark and rising tide

The storm has blown this great big beauty down
The branches all confusion on the ground
I've watched it grow and thought I knew it well
And I never dreamed I'd see the day it fell

So bolt the door, seal the cracks
Close your eyes don't look back
Hold your ears tight against the roar
Someone said I should hear
Warning cries soft and clear
Whispered in the calm before the storm

Act of nature, act of God
Raging through our sedentary lives
We are on the brink
We are floundering
Spinning in this dark and rising tide

The wind came round and blew this
    place apart.....

act of God Nature

raging through
our sedentary lives
we are on the brink,
we are floundering
spinning in this dark
and rising tide

It's you and me and we are both

Alone

WORDS OF CHERYL WHEELER
BD 09

Betty Devine

122

COW PATTERN CLOTHES

Oh the sun is shining and it's one of those
Beautiful days for cow pattern clothes
And if it should rain again then I suppose
I would get water on my cow pattern clothes

So get along little doggie or I'll punch you in the nose
Then I'll dress your mother up in cow pattern clothes
Do you like the song so far don't you think it flows?
It rambles but it stops to mention cow pattern clothes

Cow pattern shirts
Cow pattern hats
Cow pattern ball gowns
Cow pattern jock straps

Cow pattern cardigans
Cow pattern knee highs
Cow pattern papal vestments
Cow pattern Levis

Cow pattern clothes
Cow pattern clothes
Cow pattern clothes
Cow pattern clothes

Cow Pattern Clothes

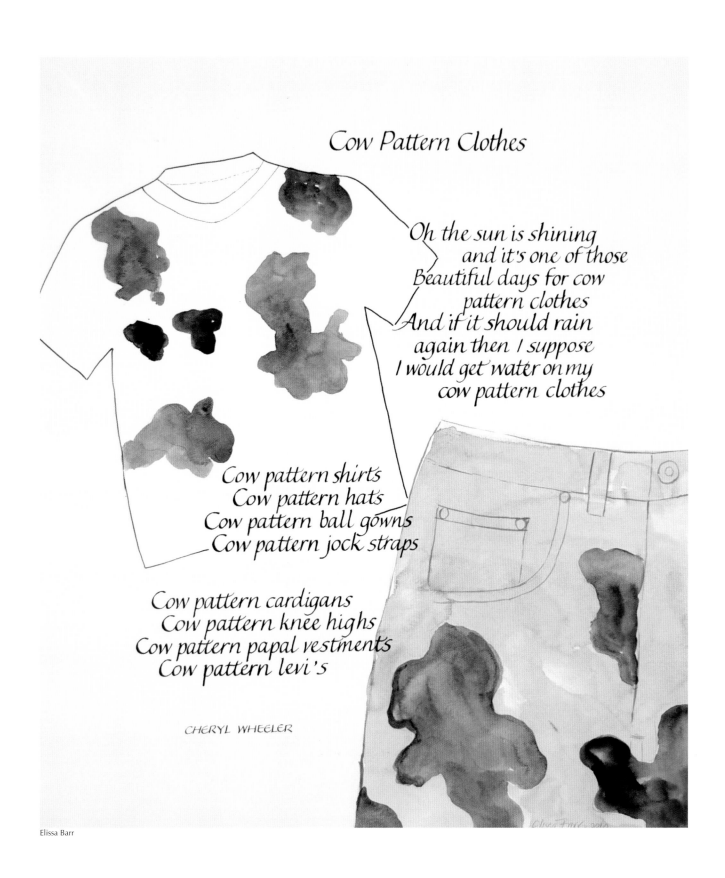

Oh the sun is shining
    and it's one of those
Beautiful days for cow
    pattern clothes
And if it should rain
    again then I suppose
I would get water on my
    cow pattern clothes

Cow pattern shirts
Cow pattern hats
Cow pattern ball gowns
Cow pattern jock straps

Cow pattern cardigans
Cow pattern knee highs
Cow pattern papal vestments
Cow pattern levi's

CHERYL WHEELER

Elissa Barr

BEHIND THE BARN

Didn't we come far - haven't we been there,
Weren't we something way back when?
Didn't we wonder - how would we come here.
Saving our dreams so they'd never end?
Oh those sweet dark nights where the warm air sings
We could close our eyes stretching still-folded wings
Waiting for the rain to cool us
Feeling like a couple of foolish young things

Weren't they good times - didn't our hearts bind,
Didn't we both find something new?
Fleeting impressions, timid expressions
Tossed in the tangle of me and you
And if I close my eyes, I can almost see
Moving through those green fields where we used to be
The shadow of a different daydream
Holding in the distance and waiting to breathe

Dusty roads, starry skies
Beating hearts, reluctant eyes
   summer rains without a storm
Nervous love behind the barn

dusty roads
starry skies
beating hearts
reluctant eyes
SUMMER · RAIN · WITHOUT · A · STORM · AND
NERVOUS · LOVE · BEHIND · THE · BARN
CHERYL WHEELER

Carol DuBosch

ONE LOVE

Everywhere I turn,
everyone is lost in this thing
'Cause something feels gone
And life is nothing like we dreamed it might be
And we don't move forward
can't move back
We hold our hands out
hoping for that

One love that's all of it
deep nights and quiet days
Long lovers, old comforts
Feel like some ball and chain

I guess we're really gettin' old
Always worrying we're wasting our time
Want somethin' new to hold
Some affair would be the perfect crime
Long roads crumble forevers fall apart
One day we don't know why we're so far… from

One love that's all of it
deep nights and quiet days
Long lovers, old comforts
Feel like some ball and chain

And if I want you, and you want me
We'll call it love though it might not be
Hearts on fire, souls in line
Oh, just to know that,
Just to feel that one more time

Seems impossible to know
what is real and what is just some restless thing
And our hearts learn slow
all the miseries bad choices bring
So is it wise or lazy,
holding tight to what you've known?
And is it brave or crazy,
searching for some…

One love that's all of it
deep nights and quiet days
Long lovers, old comforts
Feel like some ball and chain

Everything I want everyone else is this thing
'cause something felt some. It gets nothing
Like we dreamed it might like
And we don't...
So we hold our hands out hoping for
CHORUS

I guess we're really actin old
Always worrying we're wasting our time
Wantin something new to hold
Some affair would be the perfect crime
Long roads crumble, forevers fall apart
One day we don't know why we're so far from
CHORUS

And if I want
you and you want me
we'll call it love though it
might not be. Hearts on
fire, souls in time. Oh, just
to know that, just to feel
that one more time
CHORUS

Seems impossible to know
What is real and what is just some restless thing
And our hearts lean slow all the miseries bad clouds bring
So it wise or lazy holding tight to what you've known
And is it brave or crazy searching for some

That's all of it... keep nights and quiet days
Long lovers old comforts. Feel like some ball and chain.
Words by Cheryl Wheeler

ALICE

Alice works the desk at the East Bay Hotel
  in Grand Marais, Minnesota
I came in one night, She said "I loved your show"
We sat and talked on the sofa
She's on her own since her husband passed away
Some surgeon screwed up, there's nothing left to say
Now she works this desk at night and the campground by day
In a trailer by the lake until the summer blows away

She read about the job in a camping magazine
  and home was just a reminder
So she took the cat and dog, stored away her things
  left the bleakness behind her
And even now through the ache of missing him
  she's filled with wonder and far from giving in
She sees magic on the lake in the early morning light
And talking books and telling tales we sat there half the night

And she said: The more I travel the more I wanna see
My kids want some settled life for me
I don't wanna move somewhere and grow old quietly
And the more I travel, the more I wanna see

Well it's time to make a change, with winter in the wings
  and the East Bay Hotel made an offer
But she doesn't really know, 'cause there's everywhere to go
  and there's everything that traveling has taught her
Moving marches down busy city streets
Fantastic people she's privileged to meet
And she dreams about Alaska, the snow so deep and white
And that little town in Texas where there's dancing every night

And she says: The more I travel the more I wanna see
My kids want some settled life for me
I don't wanna move somewhere and grow old quietly
And the more I travel, the more I wanna see

THE MORE I TRAVEL THE MORE I WANNA SEE MY KIDS WANT SOME SETTLED LIFE FOR ME I DON'T WANNA MOVE SOMEWHERE AND GROW OLD QUIETLY

ALICE by Cheryl Wheeler

D. Flattery '09

Dave Flattery

YOU KNOW YOU WILL

She might slip out the back door
Just might be what you came for
Streetlight blinkin' shinin'
You like pullin' the line in

You know you will, you know you can
No matter where, no matter when
The cards will fall, fall where they may
You've seen it all, and anyway...

Sad part, you're gonna find out
Her heart wasn't a hide out
Once she's cruisin' the inside
You'll be hitchin' a new ride

You know you will, you know you can
No matter where, no matter when
The cards will fall, fall where they may
You've seen it all, and anyway...

Mercy how the days go by, the sweet anticipation
Love is just an alibi for your preoccupation

Hard times back on the home front
Bee lines, here come the new hunt
Love lorn seems like a pastime
Once more just like the last time

You know you will, you know you can
No matter where, no matter when
The cards will fall, fall where they may
You've seen it all, and anyway...

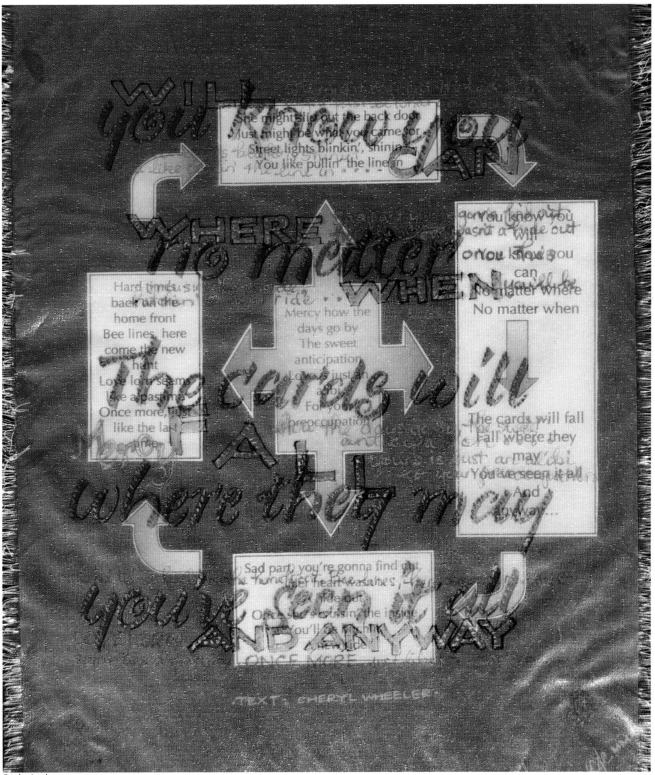

Carolyn Lueders

WHITE CAT

I was a white cat once
But when I roll around I get all gray and brown
And it does not make sense
to waste a busy day licking the dirt away
And I have staff for that, sent here to serve the cat
I let my fur get gray and then I dock their pay

It's a brand new morning as I stretch and arise
Amble over to the table, little nibble on the kibble
Shred a little sofa as I open my eyes
Yes I got ratted, matted, messed up hair
This verbal fur ball does not care
I want to be The Lord Of The Fleas
I saunter and I do what I please
So if you need to see the key to be ungroomed
You just stay tuned to this Maine Coon

I was in the garden, taking the sun
Checking out the bugs, musta rolled on one
So I got this slug bug stuck to my fur real good
But I didn't really mind, just a little bit o' slime
I'll find it later, you know, scratching my back
Be glad I saved it, make a nice little snack
I went inside, I swear the staff went insane
Running with the comb and scissors,
  screaming my name

But I give 'em the quick slip, I don't make a sound
I get onto their outfits and roll all around
My fur looks bad to me, all gray and askew
I think my staff should be displayin' it too
And they got this two bit sand pit
  they want me to use
Sometimes I don't mind, sometimes I refuse
Hey I am me, I'm free, independence rocks
This ain't no new craze to find ways
  to think outside the box

I'm really messy hey hey I like to be
And they're so testy all day at the sight o' me
Just as all work and no play wasn't meant to be
They sacrifice to feng-shui their joie de vivre
I was a white cat, I was a white cat
I was a white cat once

WHITE CAT

I WAS A WHITE CAT ONCE BUT WHEN I ROLL AROUND I GET ALL GRAY AND BROWN
AND IT DOES NOT MAKE SENSE TO WASTE A BUSY DAY LICKING THE DIRT AWAY
AND I HAVE STAFF FOR THAT, SENT HERE TO SERVE THE CAT
I LET MY FUR GET GRAY AND THEN I DOCK THEIR PAY

IT'S A BRAND NEW MORNING AS I STRETCH AND ARISE
AMBLE OVER TO THE TABLE, LITTLE NIBBLE ON THE KIBBLE
SHRED A LITTLE SOFA AS I OPEN MY EYES
YES, I GOT RATTED, MATTED, MESSED UP HAIR
THIS VERBAL FUR BALL DOES NOT CARE
I WANT TO BE THE LORD OF THE FLEAS, I SAUNTER AND I DO WHAT I PLEASE
SO IF YOU NEED TO SEE THE KEY TO BE UNGROOMED
YOU JUST STAY TUNED TO THIS MAINE COON

I WAS IN THE GARDEN, TAKING THE SUN
CHECKING OUT THE BUGS, MUSTA ROLLED ON ONE
SO I GOT THIS SLUG BUG STUCK TO MY FUR REAL GOOD
BUT I DIDN'T REALLY MIND, JUST A LITTLE BIT O'SLIME
I'LL FIND IT LATER, YOU KNOW, SCRATCHING MY BACK
BE GLAD I SAVED IT, MAKE A NICE LITTLE SNACK
I WENT INSIDE, I SWEAR THE STAFF WENT INSANE
RUNNING WITH THE COMB AND SCISSORS, SCREAMING MY NAME

(BUT I GIVE 'EM THE QUICK SLIP I DON'T MAKE A SOUND
I GET ONTO THEIR OUTFITS AND ROLL ALL AROUND
MY FUR LOOKS BAD TO ME ALL GRAY AND ASKEW
I THINK MY STAFF SHOULD BE DISPLAYIN' IT TOO
AND THEY GOT THIS TWO BIT SAND PIT THEY WANT ME TO USE
SOMETIMES I DON'T MIND, SOMETIMES I REFUSE
HEY I AM ME, I'M FREE, INDEPENDENCE ROCKS
THIS AIN'T NO NEW CRAZE TO FIND WAYS TO THINK OUTSIDE THE BOX

I'M REALLY MESSY HEY HEY I LIKE TO BE
AND THEY'RE SO TESTY ALL DAY AT THE SIGHT O' ME
JUST AS ALL WORK AND NO PLAY WASN'T MEANT TO BE
THEY SACRIFICE TO FENG-SHUI THEIR JOIE DE VIVRE
I WAS A WHITE CAT, I WAS A WHITE CAT, I WAS A WHITE CAT ONCE

WORDS & MUSIC BY CHERYL WHEELER
SCRIBE MARCIA FRIEDMAN FEB 2010

Marcia Friedman

PLEASE PLAY ME A FOLK SONG

Pour me a carrot juice and pass me a muffin,
then leave me alone.
Don't wanna read "Sing Out", don't care about nothin'
since my baby left home.

Walked off o' my job with the union mob
Hope I won't be broke long.
I'm feelin' sad and kinda mad
Oh please play me a folk song.

Play me some Woody, Seeger, Paxton and Malvina
Barbara Allen, I Ain't a Marchin', Stewball and Corrina
Oh since you left I'm so bereft, I spend my days all choked up
Got nothin' left to lose, just cryin' in my juice
and really gettin' folked up.

PLAY ME A FOLK SONG

CHERYL WHEELER

POUR ME A CARROT JUICE AND PASS ME A MUFFIN
THEN LEAVE ME ALONE
DON'T WANNA READ "SING OUT"
DON'T CARE ABOUT NOTHIN
SINCE MY BABY LEFT HOME

WALKED OFF MY JOB WITH THE UNION MOB
HOPE I WON'T BE BROKE LONG
I'M FEELING SAD AND KINDA MAD
OH PLEASE PLAY ME A FOLK SONG

PLAY ME SOME WOODY, SEEGER
PAXTON AND MALVINA
BARBARA ALLEN, I AIN'T MARCHIN', STEWBALL
AND CORRINA
OH SINCE YOU LEFT I'M SO BEREFT
SPEND MY DAYS ALL CHOKED UP
GOT NOTHIN' LEFT TO LOSE JUST CRYING IN MY JUICE
AND REALLY GETTING FOLKED UP.

C. C. Sadler

ALL THE LIVE LONG DAY

The sun is shinin', makin' this room so bright
And the cats are sleepin', right up on the table,
Breakin' all the rules in plain sight
There's a cloud colored moon floatin' in the blue
Not waitin' for the sun to go away
I just wish I could walk with you and talk with you
All the live long day

We never really had a winter, it never came and now it's gone
And the days grow longer, like a late night road
Like the odds you'll come back home
But I don't mind wasting my time
Waitin' for the ache to go away
I don't mind telling you it's what I do
All the live long day

All the live long day, I wonder what I'll do
I don't see no way, of getting over you

The boys were in the back field, sortin' out the who and when
It's like cat graffiti, but they read it with their nose
And it's written from the other end
Though James takes it in with a different spin
He likes to read the Sniff and Spray
It's just them and me, and my ennui
All the live long day

All the live long day, I wonder what I'll do
I don't see no way, of getting over you

 I was watchin' the sunset, wishin' you were watchin' too
Through the winter branches,
Drop jaw red, Maxfield Parrish blue
Then a windy night with the stars so bright
The trees just bow and sway
I been close to blue and missing you
All the live long day

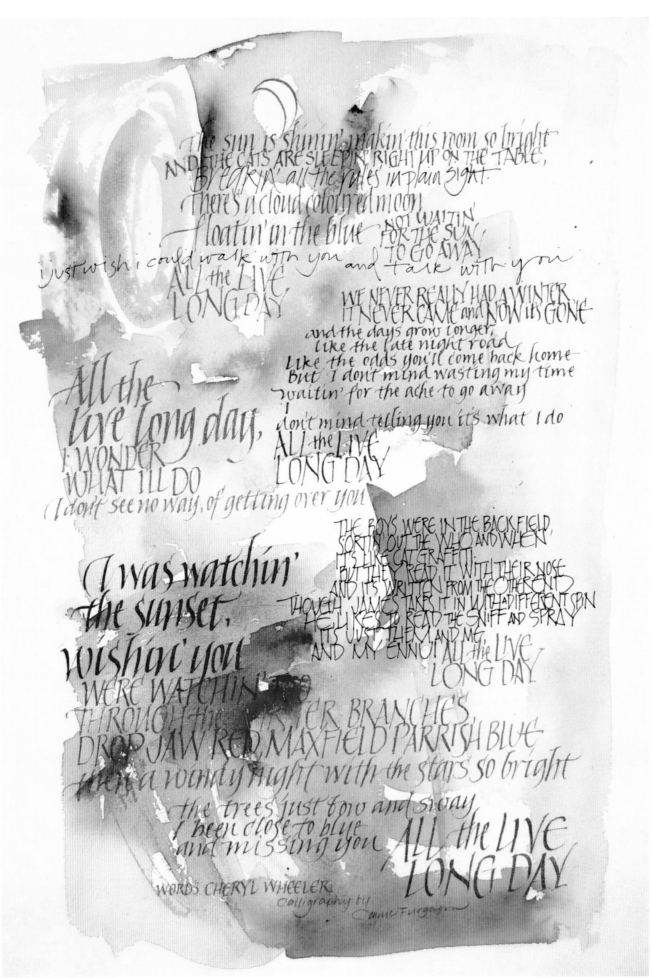

The sun is shinin' makin' this room so bright
AND THE CATS ARE SLEEPIN' RIGHT UP ON THE TABLE,
BREAKIN' all the rules in plain sight.
There's a cloud colored moon
floatin' in the blue NOT WAITIN'
FOR THE SUN
TO GO AWAY
I just wish i could walk with you and talk with you
ALL the LIVE
LONG DAY WE NEVER REALLY HAD A WINTER
IT NEVER CAME and NOW its GONE
and the days grow longer,
like the late night road
Like the odds you'll come back home
But i don't mind wasting my time
waitin' for the ache to go away

All the
live long day,
I WONDER
WHAT ILL DO
(I don't see no way, of getting over you

i don't mind telling you it's what i do
ALL the LIVE
LONG DAY

THE BOYS WERE IN THE BACK FIELD,
SORTIN OUT THE WHO AND WHEN,
ITS LIKE CAT GRAFFITI
BUT THEY READ IT WITH THEIR NOSE
I was watchin' AND ITS WRITTEN FROM THE OTHER END
the sunset, THOUGH JAMES TAKES IT IN WITH A DIFFERENT SPIN
wishin' you HE LIKES TO READ THE SNIFF AND SPRAY
WERE WATCHIN' TOO ITS JUST THEM, AND ME
THROUGH the WINTER BRANCHES AND MY ENNOT ALL the LIVE
DROP JAW RED, MAXFIELD PARRISH BLUE LONG DAY
then a windy night with the stars so bright
the trees just bow and sway
I been close to blue
and missing you ALL the LIVE
LONG DAY

WORDS CHERYL WHEELER
calligraphy by
Connie Furgason

Connie Furgason

FURTHER AND FURTHER AWAY

I can see the place where I came from
I can hear those sounds right now
I can find the paths I used to run
And believe I still know how

Then I shake my head
clearing my vision
I keep those scenes at bay
And I can see the place
where I came from
Slipping further and further away

And I can feel the way I used to feel
When the world was small and green
And you sang a song of soft appeal
And I curled into my dream

Then I shake my head
clearing my vision
I keep those scenes at bay
And I can feel the way I used to feel
Slipping further and further away

Time keeps moving
faster and faster
I'm not losing track
I'm afraid that something's forgotten
So I keep looking back

I can hear the songs you used to sing
I can swear I won't let go
You were strong
and you knew everything
That was all I had to know

Then I shake my head,
clearing my vision
I keep those scenes at bay
And I can hear the songs
you used to sing
Slipping further and further away

I can see the place where I came from
I can hear those sounds right now
I can find the paths I used to run
And believe I still know how

Then I shake my head,
clearing my vision
I keep those scenes at bay
And I can see the place
where I came from
Slipping further and further
away

And I can feel the way I used to feel
When the world was small and green
And you sang a song of soft appeal
And I curled into my dream

Then I shake my head, clearing my vision
I keep those scenes at bay · And I can feel
the way I used to feel
Slipping further and further away

Time keeps moving faster and faster · I'm not losing track
I'm afraid that something's forgotten · So I keep looking back

I can hear the songs you used to sing · I can swear I won't let go
You were strong and you knew everything · That was all I had to know

Then I shake my head,
clearing my vision
I keep those scenes at bay
And I can hear the songs you used to sing
Slipping further and further away

Carol Pallesen

ONE STEP AT A TIME

I'm all right, I'll get by
Hold my own, tell you why
Hard times come, hard times go
We're still here, high or low

I'm gonna take one step at a time,
Gonna keep walking walking walking
Everything gonna be fine, I know it will

I know you're sad, look at yourself
But turning like that, how does that help?
Every thought that crosses your head
Doesn't have to be heard, doesn't need to be said

I'm gonna take one step at a time,
Gonna keep walking walking walking
Everything gonna be fine, I know it will

Next time try the knob
  before you break my door down
Before you deal me such a clumsy blow
I could build a wall with all this faith you tore down
If I could see where all the pieces go

Some days roll like a beautiful sea
Till the light comes down through the moonlit trees
Maybe we'll win, maybe we won't
Some days fly, some days don't

I'm gonna take one step at a time,
Gonna keep walking walking walking
Everything gonna be fine, I know it will

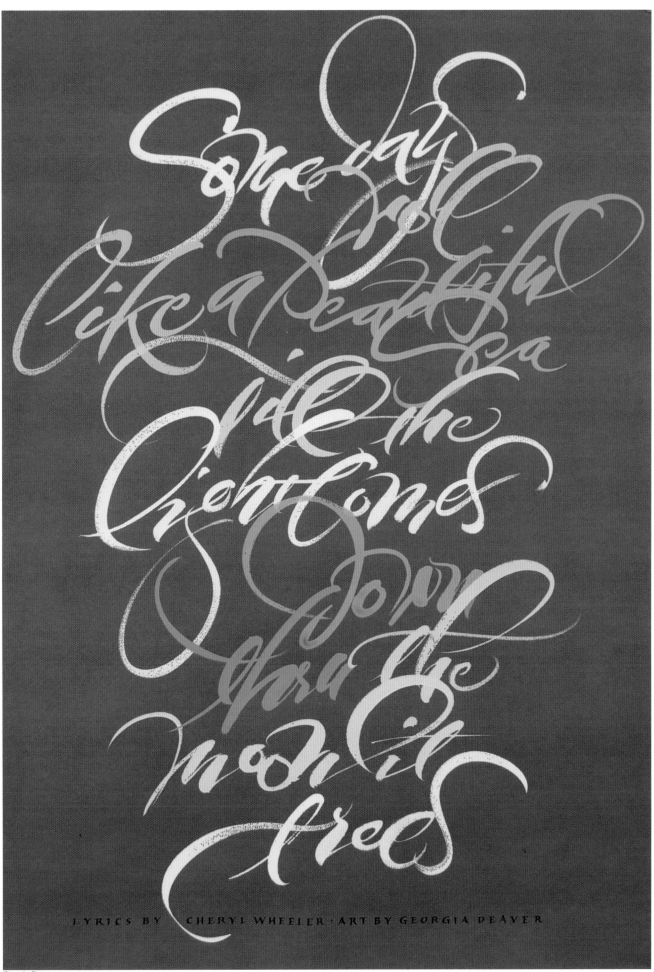

LYRICS BY CHERYL WHEELER · ART BY GEORGIA DEAVER

Georgia Deaver

POTATO

They're red, they're white, they're brown
They get that way underground
There can't be much to do
So now they have blue ones too

We don't care what they look like, we'll eat them
Any way they can fit on our plate
Every way we can conjure to heat them
We're delighted and think they're just great

Potato potato potato po
Tatopo tatopo tatopo ta
Topota topota topota to
Potato potato potato

Sometimes we ditch the skin
To eat what it's holding in
Sometimes we'd rather please
Have just the outside with cheese

They have eyes but they do not have faces
I don't know if their feelings get hurt
By just hanging around in dark places
Where they only can stare at the dirt

I guess the use is scant
For other parts of the plant
But that which grows in view
Is eating potato too

I imagine them under their acres
Out in Idaho and up in Maine
Maybe wondering if they'll be bakers
Or knishes or latkes or plain

They're red, they're white, they're brown
They get that way underground
There can't be much to do
So now they have blue ones too

We don't care what they look like we'll eat them
Any way they can fit on our plate
Every way we can conjure to heat them
We're delighted and think they just great
CHORUS
Sometimes we ditch the skin
To eat what it's holding in
Sometimes we'd rather please
Have just the outside with cheese

POTATO

PO TA TO PO TA TO PO TA TO PO
TA TO PO TA TO PO TA TO PO TA
TO PO TA TO PO TA TO PO TA TO
PO TA TO PO TA TO PO TA TO

They have eyes but they do not have faces
I don't know if their feelings get hurt
By just hanging around in dark places
Where they only can stare at the dirt

I guess the use is scant
For other parts of the plant
But that which grows in view
Is eating potato too

I imagine them under their acres
Out in Idaho and up in Maine
Maybe wondering if they'll be bakers
Or knishes or latkes or plain

Carole Roy

LOVELY RIDE

All night long,
pretty little song keeps rollin'
through my head
I can't read,
I can't sleep, just goin'
through this tune instead
I think about the way you make me feel so good
Don't know if I told you
but I know I should

Wagging tail, winding trail
"Leaves no step has trodden black" *
Evening light, winter white
Cardinals shine in the pine out back
Now inside this moment it occurs to me
Everything is just as it's supposed to be

When the cold snow blows
Or the hot sun shows no mercy
Count me in
Steeper climbs, harder times
are mostly
Just now and then
Raise your glass to the side by side
I must say it's a lovely ride

*the quoted line is from Robert Frost's "The Road Not Taken"
In the poem, it's HAD trodden, but the
point is to evoke the sense of – how my choices led me here – as
well as the solitary nature of our woods walk.

ALL NIGHT LONG,
PRETTY LITTLE SONG KEEPS ROLLIN'
THROUGH MY HEAD
I CAN'T READ,
I CAN'T SLEEP, JUST GOIN'
THROUGH THIS TUNE INSTEAD
I THINK ABOUT THE WAY YOU MAKE ME FEEL SO GOOD
DON'T KNOW IF I TOLD YOU BUT I KNOW I SHOULD

WAGGING TAIL, WINDING TRAIL
"LEAVES NO STEP HAS TRODDEN BLACK"
EVENING LIGHT, WINTER WHITE
CARDINALS SHINE IN THE PINE OUT BACK
NOW INSIDE THIS MOMENT IT OCCURS TO ME
EVERYTHING IS JUST AS IT'S SUPPOSED TO BE

WHEN THE COLD SNOW BLOWS
OR THE HOT SUN SHOWS NO MERCY
COUNT ME IN
STEEPER CLIMBS, HARDER TIMES
ARE MOSTLY
JUST NOW AND THEN
RAISE YOUR GLASS TO THE SIDE BY SIDE
I MUST SAY IT'S A LOVELY RIDE

LOVELY
RIDE

ALL NIGHT LONG
PRETTY LITTLE SONG KEEPS ROLLIN'
THROUGH MY HEAD

LYRICS AND MUSIC BY CHERYL WHEELER

M. SCHNEIDER, 2010

Marcy Schneider

BEV AND ERIN ALLEN

Bev Allen lives in Langley, British Columbia with her family. She has been a calligraphy and book arts student for 32 years and a teacher of both for about 20 years.
Her daughter, Erin, is a portrait and multimedia artist. They often collaborate on art work.
http://thedragonscribe.blogspot.com
www.erinallen.com

GAIL VICK (ANNIE) BARNHARDT

Since receiving a BFA in Graphic Design and MFA in Painting/Printmaking from Rochester Institute of Technology (RIT), I have shifted from the business of design to the art of calligraphy and teaching. I now find myself moving toward painting, drawing and the drawing of letters - and always delighting in new learning.

My teaching experiences range from the university level at RIT to public school Artist-in-Residence to Museum school and Adult Education classes. I have been privileged to teach "Design" with Marijo Carney at seven International Conferences and at many workshops. I have also taught solo workshops with an emphasis on pencil-drawn Roman letterforms.

My work has been exhibited widely and published in professional journals and books. I was honored to be the recipient of the 2008 Newberry Library Purchase prize.

I am excited to be opening a studio in a new community arts center, the Moose Exchange, in Bloomsburg, where I will teach classes and paint!

ELISSA BARR

Elissa Barr has studied calligraphy with Reggie Ezell, Ward Dunham, Shel Bassel, Nancy Culmone, and many other noted calligraphers since receiving her B.A. from Simmons College in Natural Science Illustration. Her themes encompass Hebrew and English language characters, and her work ranges from historically accurate letter forms to calligraphic abstracts and intricate geometric executions. She co-founded Masscribes, was Operations Manager of "2001: A Calligraphic Odyssey," Co-Director of Odyssey 2010, the Thirtieth International Gathering of Lettering Artists and is on the board of the Foundation for the Calligraphic Arts. She is also an avid collector of small pieces of paper, which she patiently stacks in precarious piles throughout her otherwise immaculate studio. One wonders what she might someday do with them.
Contact Elissa at: penpusherink@gmail.com

GEMMA BLACK

Gemma is a distinguished Australian calligrapher, decorative paper artist and civil marriage celebrant. Gemma recently moved to Tasmania from Canberra and enjoys the thriving creative arts community there. For over twenty years her work has encompassed regular commissions from both the public and private sectors throughout the country. Gemma is interested in formal penmanship, research and exploration into text as image and text as calligraphy. In 1986 Gemma was one of three friends who founded the Canberra Calligraphy Society which today is still a strong and wonderful group of friends who share a common passion for letters.

Awarded a Winston Churchill Memorial Trust Fellowship in 1991 to study teaching calligraphy in Europe, Gemma enjoys learning, teaching and producing calligraphic artworks. She was elected as a Guild Member of the Australian Society of Calligraphers in 1993. In 1997 Gemma achieved the status of CLAS Fellow of the Calligraphy and Lettering Arts Society, United Kingdom and in 2002 she was elected as a CLAS Honoured Fellow.

Quite simply Gemma loves letter forms and her creative journey has seen her study with highly skilled calligraphers both nationally and internationally. She has also studied watercolour painting, printmaking and bookbinding.

Please visit Gemma's website for more information: www.pcug.org.au/~gblack or http://canberragem.blogspot.com/ or email Gemma with a query or request to: gblack@pcug.org.au

PAT BLAIR

Pat has been a professional calligrapher for 24 years, and currently holds the position of Chief Calligrapher at The White House in Washington, DC.

Her work has been published in Letter Arts Review, The Calligrapher's Engagement Calendar, Scripsit, Martha Stewart Weddings, and Tabellae Insatae. Sharing and teaching what she loves is a high priority, and she teaches at the Loudoun Academy of the Arts in Virginia, and has been on the faculty of several International Calligraphy Conferences. Pat has served two years as President of the Washington Calligrapher's Guild, been Chairperson of The Graceful Envelope Contest, and has been Co-Director of Letterforum, the 26th International Calligraphy Conference.

Pat's love of pointed pen lettering led her to her study of Copperplate and Spencerian letterforms. The International Association of Master Penman and Engrossers recently awarded her the honor "Master Penman" for her work in this area.

JAN BOYD

Jan was born and raised in Seattle, Washington, earned her Masters in Social Work at the University of Washington, and migrated East. She settled in Boston and worked as a social worker for ten years, first as a caseworker with Children's Protective Services and later as director of a residential treatment facility for adolescent girls. She took evening calligraphy classes for enjoyment and relaxation – to have, as counterpoint to her day job, an activity with immediately controllable and observable products.

She met and married Tom, and they started a family with surprise twins, accurately counted only minutes before delivery. Jan's plan to return to her job with one baby became instantly unfeasible with two, so she embraced new roles as mother and part-time calligrapher.

Her business burgeoned as the children (and a third, four years younger) grew and started school. They are grown now, done with college and independent, and Jan's business, Jan Boyd Calligraphy is an established and flourishing company hand-creating invitations, envelopes, seating scrolls, etc., for weddings, and diplomas, certificates and awards for corporate clients.

In April 2008, Jan was chosen to create a means of artistically honoring all self- identified victims of abuse by clergy within the Boston Archdiocese. She created a hand lettered book featuring the first names of those 1500 victims, which was presented to Pope Benedict XVI in Washington, DC by Cardinal Sean O'Malley and five abuse victims. The book powerfully represented all victims who could not otherwise attend that historic meeting.
Contact Jan at www.janboyd.com

ANNIE CICALE

The world of books and writing has captivated Annie Cicale since she was a child. After a short career as a chemical engineer, she turned to the visual arts, specializing in painting, printmaking and drawing. The visual qualities of writing became her subject matter when she discovered the expressive power of the calligraphic forms. She finds that as she works, she is constantly trying to figure out how she would explain her ideas to a class. She has an MFA in graphic design and teaches calligraphy, drawing and painting for calligraphy guilds throughout the United States and Canada, and has taught at most of the international conferences. She is the author of The Art and Craft of Hand Lettering, a 2004 publication of Lark Books.

Annie Cicale 204 Arcadian Ct. Fairview, NC 28730   828-628-3116
e-mail: alphaannie@att.net
website: cicaletteringdesign.com

BARBARA CLOSE

Barbara has been a free-lance calligrapher, graphic designer, instructor for a number of years. She has taught many classes and workshops in various cities in California, and across the country and Canada. She also taught classes for the extension program at Calif. State University, Long Beach and Calif. State University, Fullerton. Currently she is teaching a year-long course in Calligraphy at her Studio in Santa Ana, CA. She thoroughly enjoys teaching a variety of classes that range from studies of many calligraphic styles to other unique classes that involve her creative passion.

Her work can be seen in calligraphic Calendars, the Artful Letter Calligrapher's Engagement Calendars and SfC's Artful Book of Days Calendar. She has exhibited her work in many juried shows in California and throughout the U.S. Barbara also participates and teaches at several international calligraphy conferences throughout the U.S .and has studied with many renowned calligraphers. She continues to be an active member of the Society for Calligraphy, Southern California and currently is serving as Past President and Public Relations Chair. She has designed several greeting cards for Marcel Schurman Co. and has also designed the logo for Somerset Studio magazine. She was a featured artist several times. She has also designed a font cartridge for the die-cut machine from ProvoCraft – the Cricut. It's called "The Calligraphy Collection". Her love of lettering and design continues to show in her work.

HARVEST CRITTENDEN

Harvest has been a professional lettering artist for more than 30 years. Her focus has been an in-depth study of the Sacred Arts of the Renaissance where faith, work, art and home were never considered separate but one. Harvest specializes in illuminating words that inspire and support our ever-changing world. Harvest has made several trips to Italy to continue that study, and founded Acorn Arts with that in mind. She has included other artists and calligraphers that share that vision. Together they hope to make a meaningful contribution and give a percentage of all profits to charity. Harvest is a past recipient of the Marjorie Pavelich Calligraphy Grant. She teaches at the Birmingham Bloomfield Art Center and Hollander's School of Book and Paper Arts. She is the past President of the Michigan Association of Calligraphers. She has taught workshops around the country and has been invited to teach at six International Conferences of Lettering Arts. Harvest has been published several times and has exhibited in numerous juried shows. Her work is in museums and private collections around the world. Harvest also teaches for the St. Michael's Institute of Sacred Arts and The Religious Sisters of Mercy. Harvest will receive the high honor of being inducted as a Master Penman by the International Association of Master Penman, Engrossers and Teachers of Handwriting, at their annual convention. Harvest lives with her husband, Larry in a charming little town in Michigan.
You can see her work at www.acornarts.org

MARY ANN DAVID

Mary Ann is an Oregonian who has been doing her beloved calligraphy for twenty years. She has studied with most of the great calligraphers of our time and continues to learn! Fran Strom, Inga Dubay and Carol DuBosch have been her most valued muses. She incorporates her favorite activities (family, gardening and cooking) into her work with fascinating results.

GEORGIA DEAVER

Georgia found her calling as an artist while she was a teenager growing up in San Jose, CA. Her love of experimentation with line and color had led Georgia down a vibrant, award winning path as a lettering artist and illustrator. She has run her own studio in San Francisco since 1984, executing the full gamut of jobs - from hand lettered envelopes to corporate signage on the gleaming hulls of airplanes. Georgia is a nominated member of the distinguished Society of Scribes and Illuminators, an advisory board member of the Western Art Directors Club and a former board member of the San Francisco Society of Illustrators. Georgia's art has been exhibited both nationally and internationally and has won her numerous awards from such organizations as Communication Arts and The New York Type Director's Club, among others.
To view her website, see www.georgiadeaver.com

BETTY DEVINE

Betty began her study of lettering in the early 1980's and was particularly influenced by her studies in Portland, OR with Jaki Svaren, Fran Strom and Joyce Graff. Later, she enjoyed studying with Reggie Ezell in his yearlong class. From the beginning, she found herself drawn to the art of illuminated letters and has spent much time in the ensuing years in the study of medieval manuscripts and the techniques and materials used to produce them. While she has focused largely upon jewelry design for the past 15 years, her forays back into the world of letters generally involve the use of gold whenever possible.

KRISTEN DOTY

Kristen has a passion for calligraphy, drawing and painting. She obtained and continues her art education by taking classes and workshops in the US, Canada and Europe, and by studying art books, magazines and originals in galleries and museums.

Her original works have been in juried exhibits and her paintings, illustrations and lettering have been published in magazines and books, and as prints, posters, greeting cards, logos and book titles.

Recently, her artwork is included in the new book, Strokes of Genius 2, The Best of Drawing Light & Shadow, edited by Rachel Rubin Wolf, published by NorthLight Books and she was commissioned to do the illustration, calligraphy and design of the US Secretary of State's holiday card.

She enjoys sharing her passion by teaching workshops across the country and abroad. Her teaching emphasis is to promote learning in a fun, encouraging and relaxed atmosphere while also building a solid knowledge of techniques and developing skills students can utilize and integrate in their own work.
To view her work, please visit: www.kristendoty.com
E-mail: contactkd@kristendoty.com
Mailing Address: PO Box 302, Chehalis, WA 98532

CAROL ERICKSON DUBOSCH

Carol teaches calligraphy full-time in Portland, Oregon. She is passionate about sharing her knowledge and skills. She has taught calligraphy, and related classes throughout the country and at several International Conferences. When not in the classroom, Carol does free-lance calligraphy and commissions. Carol was Director of the 1987 and 1991 International Calligraphy Conferences held in Portland, Oregon.
Contact: Carol DuBosch 1738 NW 143 Avenue Portland, Oregon 97229
503-629-0161
abcdubosch@verizon.net

WARD DUNHAM

Ward is a master calligrapher who has been practicing calligraphy and design for over 40 years. He has studied, exhibited, and taught internationally. While he loves all calligraphic hands, he is especially fond of the blackletter (or gothic) hands, gothic images, and the history of the late middle ages. He is also fond of graceful & practical calligraphy tools, fountain pens with italic nibs, and sharp knives. Ward and his partner Linnea Lundquist have merged their love of calligraphy to form Atelier Gargoyle, a studio that specializes in the crafts related to calligraphy, handwriting, type design, and the graphic arts.
www.AtelierGargoyle.com

LISA ENGELBRECHT

Lisa started making art and letters to avoid having a real job and now passionately pursues lettering of all types on all surfaces. She's a lettering and multi- media artist and instructor in calligraphy and mixed media. Lisa teaches workshops and classes internationally specializing in lettering on fabric, experimental lettering and the creative process.

Her unique style has landed her on the faculty of ten international lettering conferences and she teaches at collage, quilting and alternative arts conferences nationwide. In 2006 Lisa introduced new multi- media classes at the International Quilt Show in Houston, Texas. She is interested not only in classical letterforms but also alternative surfaces for lettering and current street influences on modern calligraphy. Lisa has never followed the rules of the lettering art world and prides herself on this fact. She has translated this attitude to her work and teaching methods. She is a frequent contributor to Somerset Studios and her work on fabric was featured on the covers of Legacies and Quilting Arts magazines. She is currently creating a grafitti diversion program in her city of Long Beach, California and has designed her first tattoo!

Lisa is also a freelance lettering artist for American Greetings AND she is the author of the best selling book from Rockport Publishing, <u>Modern Mark Making, from Classic Calligraphy to Hip Lettering</u>. (The paperback version will be out soon with a brand new title - <u>Modern Calligraphy and Hand Lettering </u>- but the same goodness inside!)

Her new book will be called <u>Really Easy Watercolor Flowers and Calligraphy</u>, a handbook to simple methods to make stunning florals and combine them with lettering.

To contact Lisa:
www.lisaengelbrecht.com
www.lisaletters.blogspot.com
Flickr Photo site link is www.flickr.com/photos/25736261@N00/

DAVE FLATTERY

I want to first thank Cheryl for writing the music I have loved for a long time now, and Aimee and Carole for inviting me to be a part of this project. It is really an honor to have my work seen in the same collection with so many artists I have admired, many of whom I have had as teachers. The calligraphic community is like no other I have known. It is a most sharing and welcoming group. It is a world where all levels of skill come together to teach and help one another, a microcosm of how the world SHOULD be.

My first calligraphy class was in 1978. It was one class of one semester of a commercial art course. I only finished two years of that four year program. When I realized that I couldn't afford to finish all four years I broke from the "suggested" curriculum and took all studio classes the second year, much to the horror of my fellow students. I had a ball that year.

Somehow calligraphy embedded itself in my mind and I have worked to do the best I could with it ever since. I was, like many other calligraphers, on my own with it for about the next ten years. Libraries had little reference, the internet was nonexistent, and I never was fortunate enough to come across any other calligraphers or guilds. When I moved back to Massachusetts I found Gerry Jackson Kerdok at the Worcester Art Museum. She was my second calligraphy teacher. She helped fix some of my self taught bad habits. But more importantly she introduced me to Masscribes and C.J. Kennedy who introduced me to Cyberscribes. Cyberscribes opened up a whole world, literally, of teachers. I could never fully express my gratitude to them for their generosity, warmth and encouragement.

For the amount of years I have been practicing calligraphy I probably should be much better at it. Calligraphy is still a hobby for me. I'm still known more as Dave, the mailman from Massachusetts, and I'm OK with that.

MARCIA FRIEDMAN

Marcia has been a professional graphic designer and calligrapher for over 30 years. A graduate of the California College of Arts & Crafts, she has designed numerous publications (including the Friends of Calligraphy Alphabet), brochures, corporate identity programs, etc. through her design business, Visual Solutions. She is a senior designer for O'Reilly Media, Inc. and teaches lettering arts and papercrafts in the San Francisco Bay Area. Marcia has been on the faculty of three international calligraphy conferences and is a recovering director of the 2000 conference Experiment: Concepts in Calligraphy. In her spare time she is addicted to scrapbooking, buying too much paper and photographing her parakeets. The best way to reach her is email: marcia@oreilly.com. A website is in the works.

CONNIE FURGASON

Connie had a hint of her destiny as a lettering artist when she won the silver spoon award for penmanship in grade 5. Her university background in art and english provided the foundation for her love of words and letters. She has been teaching classes and workshops across Canada and the US since 1981. Her work has been published in "ABC Canada", "The Spirit of Calligraphy", Speedball Handbook 23rd Edition", and "The Art and Craft of Hand Lettering". Ongoing work includes lettering and illustration for the commercial card and print industry as well as private commissions. She was director of "Pen-Ultima '99", the 19th International Calligraphy Conference in Lethbridge, Alberta and two regional conferences. She has also been on faculty at several international conferences. Web/Email info. Contact: furgasonc@hotmail.com or conniefurgason.com

NANCY GALLIGAN

Nancy has been a student of calligraphy for a long time. She is a long-time, active member of Masscribes. In addition to all of the individuals she has done lettering jobs for, she can claim as continuing clients, Wellesley College and Boston College. Her work has been entered in juried and non-juried shows in Massachusetts and at the DeCordova Museum School where she is a student. Nancy has been influenced and inspired by many teachers, calligraphers, artists, poets, and writers but none of these more important than her fellow students at DeCordova on Tuesday mornings.

MIKE GOLD

Mike is a senior lettering designer at American Greetings in Cleveland, OH, where he's worked the past 17 years. As part of his freelance business, abbeygold design, he has done lettering-centered design and art work for clients around the country. Mike has an M.A. in Visual Communications and thirty years experience as a commercial artist. Before Cleveland, he lived two years in New Mexico, where the landscape and the art and the people he met influenced his life thereafter. Mike has taught around the country and at two international calligraphy conferences with his friend Judy Melvin. Collaboration has been a feature of much of his personal work. He especially cherishes his nearly 20-year involvement with Scribes 8, a collaborative group based in New Mexico. Teaching calligraphy to inmates at a women's prison is, to date, his most unusual teaching experience. Mike's work has been included in numerous Letter Arts Review annuals since 1991.

Contact info:
Mailing address: 16203 Waterford Dr. North Royalton, OH 44138
Phone: 440.582-2452(H) 216.252-7300x4639(W)
Email: abbeygold@ameritech.net (H) mike.gold@amgreetings.com (W)
Website: www.abbeygolddesign.com

JULIE GRAY

After a 40 year career in commercial art and business, Julie Gray, a graduate of the Columbus College of Art & Design, spends more time now practicing calligraphy and bookmaking. She is a member of Escribiente, the calligraphy guild in New Mexico, as well as Cyberscribes and other guilds. She has attended 12 international calligraphy conferences, and is in various handmade book, Artist Trading Card, and greeting card exchanges. Her work has been published in Bound & Lettered, Letter Arts Review, the 2004 Calligraphers Engagement Calendar, Somerset Studio, as well as various exhibits, including the NM Special Collections Library, and other local and national displays. Julie lives, loves and letters in Albuquerque, New Mexico.
She can be reached at inkster1@juno.com

JEN GROVE

Jen Grove fell for letter beauty in her teens. She saw the woodcuts in the Arthurian legends by E.B.White and would go to the library and trace and fill in every fanciful letter she could find, thinking calligraphy was drawn letters.

One day she found out that the art history teacher at Marietta College (Marietta, Ohio) taught calligraphy and that led to her being a charter member of the Marietta Calligraphy Society and down a vast road of classes and camaraderie that keeps her studying with every instructor hanging out a shingle. She is currently taking an online class with Teri Martin and a year long course called Primitive to Modern with Reggie Ezell.

After a 6 year stint as an inscription artist at Fenton Art Glass, learning to letter with 24 kt gold, she began Custom hand lettering on glass and that lead to sandblasting and engraving interests that dominate the day. She worked 3 years in the studios of AGA (Architectural Glass Art) in Louisville Kentucky. Her work is in the Glassworks Gallery in downtown Louisville where she is currently the inscription artist for hand-blown works. She is also a personalizing artist for Hadley Pottery, lettering on green-ware.

Jen exhibited a one woman show of her calligraphy for her alma mater upon the 150 anniversary of women being admitted to Marietta College called Words of the Educated Woman, Quotes of Love and Art. 30 pieces and 5 handmade books.

She taught Lettering on Glass at the 2003 international calligraphy convention "Celebrations" and for twenty years she made an appearance in every 5 and 6th grade class room in a 5 county area with a 90 minute presentation that included an introduction to the history of calligraphy and the making of an accordion fold book with decorated initial.

She is currently working on a major project in collaboration with a faculty member at Lesley College in Cambridge MA to do the broadsides for 20 poems that will be presented in a multimedia one woman show August 2010 called the Many Faces of Love.

ADAM HELLER AND TRACY MAHAFFEY

Established in 2007, Samaritan Carvers is a collaboration between Tracy Mahaffey and Adam Heller. Their approach to stone carving stems from a desire to meld words and sculpture in a seamless way.

Adam Heller began stone carving in 1997 while studying with Sister Praxedes Baxter at the Abbey of Regina Laudis in Bethlehem, CT. Adam's professional experience with lettering began in 1998 with an apprenticeship at the John Stevens Shop in Newport RI where the tradition of hand drawn brush lettering, and hand carving stone thrives (www.johnstevensshop.com). As well as producing his own work, Adam works with Karin Sprague Stone Carvers in Scituate RI - (www.karinsprague.com) and with Tracy Mahaffey of Samaritan Carvers.

Tracy Mahaffey is a professional stone carver living and working in Foster, Rhode Island. In collaboration with Adam Heller, she created Samaritan Carvers, a stone carving shop dedicated to the fine art and craftsmanship of hand carving stone with mallet and chisel.
Their work can be seen at www.samaritancarvers.com. Custom commissions are accepted.

THOMAS HOYER

Thomas has studied graphics and calligraphy with Prof. Werner Eikel in Aachen, Germany, the hometown of Charlemagne. Born in 1964, writing and creating letters has been a passion for him for more than 25 years now. Influenced by the thoughts of Hans-Joachim Burgert the visualization of a text's content is his biggest drive and the conviction that every letter is only a definition with infinite possibilities of shape.

He has worked for the Calligraphy Department of the Office of Foreign Affairs. Today he works as a freelance lettering artist for design agencies, institutions and private persons. Thomas has 18 years of teaching experience including a set of workshops for Russian type designers in Moscow summer 2009 and he travels widely throughout the U.S. and Canada giving workshops.

Schriftatelier Hoyer
Thomas Hoyer   Oranienstraße 25   52066 Aachen
+49.241.54 34 28   contact@callitype.com   www.callitype.com

ANGEL HUERTAS

I am from Boston MA. I have always loved writing, but never really knew the right way to do it.
In 2001 I came across my first calligraphy book (The Speedball Textbook) and my passion for calligraphy was born. I've never looked back. I specialize in Roundhand (spencerian, engravers script) and Blackhand, but I practice all the hands because they are all beautiful. My work has been part of two exhibits.
I also do private lettering for special occasions such as weddings, citations parties etc...

You can see some of my work on facebook under angel_huertas@live.com.

MIKE KECSEG

Mike began doing lettering when he worked as an engrosser. Since 1984 he has owned and operated Pen Graphics Studio Inc. He has been on the faculty of several international calligraphy conferences and teaches workshops throughout the country specializing in the pointed pen. He is interested in helping calligraphers make the transition from traditional pointed scripts to more expressive ones.
His work has been exhibited widely and can be seen in Letter Arts Review, Lettering Arts and the Speedball Textbook.
www.pengraphicsstudio.com

TONI KELLY

Toni is a calligrapher and painter working with watercolor and mixed media art. As a watercolorist, Toni's work reflects nature and botanical art while her mixed media art combines nature, calligraphy and collage. Her work has been accepted in jury exhibitions and can be found in local galleries and private collections. Toni has been published in Bound and Lettered for her creative books and published in Artful Blogging for her blog 'A Spattering'. She is also a volunteer for PA Audubon helping at the bird banding station on Presque Isle.

Self-employed, she works out of her home doing business as Kelly Ink Studio designing, painting and creating commissions for individuals and business clientele. She is a member of the Northwest Pennsylvania Artist Association and the Pittsburgh Guild of Calligraphers.

Toni sells her work from her studio and also online at http://kellyinkstudio.com
and her Etsy Shop, http://www.etsy.com/shop/tonikelly.
KELLY INK Studio
E-mail kellyinkstudio@verizon.net
Web Journal: http://kellyinkstudio.blogspot.com
Art, Calligraphy and Design KellyInkStudio.com
1850 East Lake Road Erie, PA 16511
814.456.4897

GERRY JACKSON KERDOK

I am primarily a student of Calligraphy and hope to be so all my life. I have been inspired by many teachers in my 33 year pursuit of letters in both workshops and conferences as well as in my 'Reggie' year. I am excited to learn more as I have really just begun.

As a teacher at The Worcester Art Museum I am humbled by the talents of my students. I think I learn more from them than I teach. I am also challenged by them to continue to grow and be more than I am at any given moment.

Lastly, I am intrigued by the movement in our Calligraphic world towards an exploration of letters as expressive marks having a life of their own. More inspiration…more excitement…more challenges.   ·
gjkerdok@gmail.com

RUTH KORCH

Ruth of Santa Cruz, California, has always had a strong love for the interplay of script and image. Her artwork has been published in books, calendars, greeting cards and posters. Her originals are in private collections across the country. Ruth has received awards and recognition in both national and international competition. She is a children's art teacher and also loves sharing her passion for beautiful letterforms by teaching calligraphy classes.

"I have always relished my role as a visual artist. My medium and style are always changing, but currently there are three categories of expression: oils, watercolor and calligraphy. I especially enjoy combining text and image. Overarching all of my work however, is a desire to leave the viewer encouraged – to create visual pathways for viewers to appreciate life's simple joys, or to be grateful for our world's breathtaking beauty." Ruth Korch
www.Ruthkorch.com

MARY LAWLER

I was genetically pre-disposed to being an artist. My mother's mother was a textiles designer and painter, her father an architect. My Father's father and his father were stone carvers. My mother was accomplished in embroidery and quilting. Her sisters were painters. I am grateful to all of them for my artistic gene. I always knew what I wanted to do; it was never a choice. The only choice I had to make was to embrace the gift and run with it or give in to fear and take a safer route. I had an even rarer gift, the encouragement and support of my family, to pursue art. Since graduating Art School I have made my living, my vocation, my career, with art. I started studying calligraphy in High School, but after a few years as a Graphic Designer, Calligraphy rose to the forefront again. Incorporating hand lettered text with type became a focus in my commercial work; books, manuscripts and broadsides became the focus of my private work. Over the years the work has shifted in style and intent, size and medium but I have never stopped studying. I continue to take classes when possible, I look, I read, I study, I learn, I teach, I learn, I practice, I live, I learn.

PATTE LEATHE

I've always loved letterforms, and coveted the funny pen in the back of the Seventeen magazine – it was an Osmiroid, and promised I too could write the beautiful forms. I finally got one in 1978, and have been buying pens, taking classes and trying to make beautiful letters ever since. This Odyssey will be my 20th conference, and I have had the opportunity to study with many wonderful artists.

Aimee introduced me to the music of Cheryl Wheeler many years ago, and we try to see her whenever she is in Hartford. Her song '75 Septembers' was especially touching to me as I thought about what my father might have thought about all the changes that have gone on since his passing, and even more meaningful as I listened to it driving back and forth to care for my Mom. Cheryl's songs are so rich in images that I 'see' them as I listen, and that is a wonderful experience. I live in West Hartford, CT with my wonderful, patient husband of 30 years, Peter. I still have that first Osmiroid pen, and it still works!
I can be reached at pLeathe@aol.com

MARTA LEGECKIS

Marta has been practicing the art of calligraphy for over 30 years. A resident of the Washington, D.C. area, Marta's clients have included the White House, the State Department, the Vice-President's office, Foundation for the Preservation of Art in Embassies (FAPE), the National Gallery and various embassies. Her specialty is the "one of a kind" award that reflects either something about the recipient or the reason for the award. One of her main clients for this type of work is the Department of the Interior. Marta is a former President, Vice-President and Workshop Chairman of the Washington Calligraphers Guild. She was also the Co-Director of Letterforum 2006. Marta's work has appeared in several issues of Scripsit, most notably in the issue "Pens & Protocol: The Calligraphy of Official Washington". Within the last few years, Marta has also begun to incorporate her watercolor paintings into her calligraphic works.

The main influences in her calligraphic journey have been Ieuan Rees, Charles Pearce and Sheila Waters.

Marta may be contacted at morkaleg@yahoo.com
(301)493-8907 Studio
(301)693-1061 Cell

LOUIS L. LEMOINE

Louis is a "Visual Magician" (designer, lettering artist and illustrator), Educator and Entertainer.
He is a Principal Graphic Designer for Walt Disney Imagineering, a division of The Walt Disney Company and also does freelance design work through his company lemoine design. He has a Master of Arts Degree in Art, with emphasis in the area of Design, from California State University at Los Angeles, and has a valid-for-life Community College teaching credential. He also is a 34 year Magician Member of Holly-wood's famous Magic Castle, a private club for magician's and magic enthusiasts. He resides in Temple City, California USA
website: www.louislemoine.com
blog: www.louislemoine.blogspot.com

CAROLYN LUEDERS

Carolyn is Unworthy (!) and grateful to Norma and Aimee for throwing her a lifeline to the calligraphy community.
She has four children and teaches classical piano.

SHERRIE LOVLER

Calligraphy has been Sherrie's passion and livelihood for over 35 years. She sells prints of her work online at www.inkmonkey.com and teaches workshops on color and design nationwide, including Ghost Ranch and four of the international calligraphy conferences. The book, Two As One, twelve calligraphic paintings of love poems between Sherrie and her boyfriend, is soon to be published. Her newest venture, making quick calligraphic sketches inspired by her own poetry, is on view at natureartandpoetry.blogspot.com.

KATHERINE MALMSTEN

A calligrapher and designer near Seattle, Washington, I have a BFA in Painting and a BA in English Literature from the University of Washington. They have proven to be an excellent (though unplanned!) background for calligraphic work; and I have since pursued specialized studies in calligraphy and lettering in both the commercial and fine art aspects.

I have particular interest in new and experimental tools, using them to create letterforms that have visual texture. Contemporary interpretations of traditional forms, using text in its visual and verbal aspects (how it looks as well as what it says), and mixing elements all find their way into my exhibit and personal pieces.

Since letterforms are my favorite subject matter, I am always looking for new ways and mediums to integrate them into my environment. I have used them on jewelry, on walls, and three-dimensional objects as well as broadsides and books. Some examples of these can be seen on my website at www.katherinemalmsten.com

TERI MARTIN

Teri was raised in Hawaii, spent most of her adult life in California and finally settled in a small artist community in Eureka Springs, AR. Her early work was in oil painting. Eventually, she was captured by the beauty and expressiveness of calligraphy. Today, she happily combines painting and lettering. Her work is licensed by many companies and can be found in the social expression industry, fabric, murals and fine art. Teri's work has been published in many guild newsletters, The Speedball Textbook and the juried annual of Letter Arts Review.
www.terimartin.com
teri@terimartin.com

ROANN MATHIAS

Roann is a mixed media artist who has specialized in calligraphy since 1980. Her calligraphic paintings are driven by an intense love of letterforms, and the beauty of color and light in nature. After receiving a master's degree in Art History, she began designing greeting cards and calendars for Conception Abbey's Printery House. Her work has been published in Letter Arts Review and Somerset Studio Magazine. Roann's calligraphy has been exhibited at the Newberry Library in Chicago, two international calligraphy conferences and other locations around the country. Currently, Roann teaches calligraphy and mixed media workshops throughout the US.
View her work on the web at www.roanndesigns.com

NORMA MCKENZIE

Norma started calligraphy with an elective while an undergrad. Several years later, with interest renewed, she began taking courses in Cambridge, MA with Sally Robertshaw. During that time the first ever conference was held in MN in 1981 and it proved to be a pivotal week that encouraged continued study both locally and at subsequent conferences. Since then, she has done commissions, her own creative work and has taught the subject in Boston and its environs. The thrill of putting letters on a good piece of paper is an ongoing process for which she is eternally grateful.

JUDY MELVIN

Judy's lifelong passion for art started with crayons and advanced to inks, paints, pens and a combination of all in mixed-media layering. She enjoyed a twelve-year career with American Greetings Corporation as a design and lettering artist where she focused on creating lettering for product, new fonts, and painting and designing countless greeting cards for the innovative Coffeehouse line. Judy teaches design, mixed-media, and brush lettering workshops throughout the US & Canada and has served as faculty of the International Lettering Conferences. She has also taught as faculty of Literally Letters, Ghost Ranch, New Mexico. Judy practices what she teaches with her unique version of fine artwork which incorporate illegible lettering layered with mixed-media. Her work has been published and exhibited throughout the USA, Canada, Austria and is in numerous collections worldwide.

AIMEE MICHAELS

Aimee began her lettering odyssey in 1986. Words and music have always been an important part of her life. This project has joined all of her passions. In the 90's, unbeknownst to any of the parties involved, there was a confluence of events that made this project possible. Aimee found Cheryl and her music, became a groupie, met other groupies and in 1997 met the love of her life. She can't thank Cheryl enough and thinks she "must've done something great to get to have", Carole.
Aimee co-founded Masscribes, was the Director of 2001: A Calligraphic Odyssey, Co-Directed Odyssey 2010 and does free lance lettering and web design. Her work has been published in The Calligrapher's Engagement Calendar and various other publications and has been included in juried and non juried exhibits.
She may be reached at aimeemichaels@verizon.net

C. A. MILLNER

C. A. is a calligrapher and mapmaker whose work can be traditional or modern, real or abstract and visually loud or quiet. She is passionate about both art forms and is ever in search of the perfect letter.

Ms. Millner has exhibited her work and taught classes in the U.S. and Europe. She has offered an ongoing class to a group of accomplished artists for over ten years and continues with her own course of studies.

J. DANIEL MOONEY

My name is J. Daniel Mooney and I reside in Quincy, Massachusetts and have a studio in Hanover, Massachusetts where I practice my passion as a lettering artist.

It is one of my life's pleasures to create art through letter form! This love affair began over 40 years ago in High School art class when I picked up my first calligraphy pen, dipped it into a bottle of ink and copied "The Boston Globe" logo in Old English.

Now, middle aged, my passion and love for letter form grows evermore. My sources of inspiration are music, literature, masters of old and the challenge of striving for perfection. I work in several mediums which are common and uncommon; modern and ancient. My art forms include gold leaf, watercolors, gouaches, various forms of wet and dry pigments, used with contemporary as well as primitive binders.

My style is markedly structured in nature which enables my creativity to flourish in color, texture and harmony. I have used my unique skill set to combine progressive and vintage disciplines to portray modern and classic themes. It is my hope that my art communicates to all who view it despite class or creed.

I am past President of Masscribes, Inc, past President of Colonial Calli-Graphics, L.L.C. I have given workshops, lessons, have had my work published and exhibited.

It is my goal as an artist to obtain the highest level of technical skill in every medium that I work, in order to communicate strongly every subject, idea and concept that I explore.

www.scribedan.com
scribedan@aol.com
Studio: 269 Hanover Street Hanover, MA 02339 781-826-7187

CHERRYL MOOTE

Cherryl has been a paper artist for over thirty years. Her specialities include bookbinding, calligraphy, and paper decorating. Cherryl has taught throughout North America and has published a number of books for paper enthusiasts. Grateful for the impact of many artistic mentors, she devotes a large part of her time to teaching, inspiring and connecting with other artists around the world.
To see samples of Cherryl's work go to her company website at www.mootepoints.com and visit the gallery section.

CAROL PALLESEN

Calligraphy is an everyday celebration for Carol Pallesen. She works, studies, and teaches in her studio, the Silent Hand Scriptorium in Reno, NV, which was established in 1981. While her first love is doing fine art calligraphy, Carol's bread-and-butter comes from commissioned work including invitations, logos, certificates, greeting cards, and original broadsides, such as the one she did for this Cheryl Wheeler book. There's something very special and magical about dipping a pen into ink and watching the letters come off the end of the nib. She wants to keep age old techniques and disciplines alive in this technological period of our lives.

Carol Pallesen
P.O. Box 9002
Reno, NV 89507
775-329-6983 phone and fax

JANE PARILLO

I began studying the art of calligraphy in 1980, after having finished two years of graduate school. One of my closest friends had given me a Shaeffer pen set as a Christmas gift . I played with it for a bit and then thought - maybe a class? The Introduction to Calligraphy class, which was "for fun" and intended to serve as a relaxing treat after a grueling couple of years, lit the fire for what has now become a lifelong passion.

In 1986 I became a member of Masscribes and my real journey began. To this day, many of my closest friends have sprung from my relationship with this guild. In 1989 I opened my studio/gallery in East Greenwich, Rhode Island and am more consumed with this art form than ever. I am honored to be part of this publication.
Please visit my website: www.janeparilloscribe.com

CAROL PERCY

Carol is a middle school counselor in Nashville, Tennessee and has enjoyed the study of lettering since the late 70's. She is a fan of Cheryl Wheeler's music and has had the opportunity to hear her in the round at The Bluebird Café in Nashville so it was exciting to learn of this book project. She chose to respond artistically to "Summer Fly" as it reflects the feelings of adolescence that she encounters in her work with young teens and the looking back on those hot summer days of her own youth. Carol especially enjoys the merging of her love of art and music in creative expression.
She may be contacted at cpercy@earthlink.net.

AMY PFLEIGER

Amy Pfleiger is a calligrapher from the Pacific Northwest.

CARL ROHRS

Carl is a calligrapher, sign painter and teacher who lives in Santa Cruz, CA.
His wife was a devoted Cheryl Wheeler fan and he tagged along.

MYRNA ROSEN

Myrna has been adjunct instructor of Lettering and Calligraphy at Carnegie Mellon University in the School of Design since 1985. She was apprentice and assistant to the late Professor of Calligraphy and Graphic design at CIT/CMU, Arnold Bank. Myrna has also been instructor of Calligraphy at the Pittsburgh Center for the Arts for the past thirty years.

Myrna has taught at many of the International Lettering Arts Conferences since their inception in 1981. She is founding and office holding member of the Calligraphy Guild of Pittsburgh. Her work has been published and exhibited nationally and internationally. She is most proud of the restoration of the marble benefactors tablets which flank the exit of the Duquesne University Chapel. Myrna's studies are on-going with masters of various aspects of the book arts as well as personal enrichment. Myrna is a devoted student of the development of the alphabet and strives to perpetuate our calligraphic heritage. At the moment Myrna has enjoyed some of the fruits of her labors in a one woman show at a Pittsburgh gallery. Aside from her husband, children and grandchildren, Myrna's passion is calligraphy in all of its aspects. She especially enjoys the rewards of teaching, which is reflected in the enthusiasm, devotion, and long term relationships she maintains with students past and present.

CAROLE ROY

Carole Roy began her calligraphic career when, at age 13, she exchanged letters in decorated envelopes with a summer friend; the five cent stamps were much less expensive than a long distance phone call. She opened her business, Calligraphy For Your Fancy in 1995 on a steady diet of wedding envelopes and invitations, seating scrolls, certificates, poems, proclamations and in the ensuing years has added artist books, paddles, walls, signs, baseballs and almost anything else that will hold on to ink or paint. She has a BFA in graphic design and letterform from UMass Dartmouth and is especially grateful to Professor Howard Glasser, who taught much more than how to wiggle a pen. Carole also learned many wonderful things from Masscribes, Inc., both in workshops, through exhibits, and by serving on the Board, currently as co-President. When you read this she will hopefully have uploaded her website to www.CalligraphyForYourFancy.com, but can also be reached at croyscribe@yahoo.com

CYNTHIA RUDOLPH

4

Cynthia grew up in the southern tier of New York State. After graduating from the University of Denver, CO with a BFA in Advertising Design, she worked for the US Army Special Services Agency in Germany. She has been a freelance artist, teacher and calligrapher and currently works at her local library. Her other interests include mixed-media jewelry, painting and fine craft. She's a member of Masscribes and past president of the Norwood Art Association. Cynthia lives in Norwood, Massachusetts with her husband Steve and they are parents of a grown daughter, Shay.

C. C. SADLER

136

C.C. is a technologist, calligrapher and lettering artist living in Sunset Beach, California.

She loves typography and drawn letterforms. Her latest enthusiasms are using watercolor with her lettering designs and Zentangles. For sanity's sake, she only approaches lettering as an avocation, never accepting payment. However, she greatly admires the many lettering artists in the L.A. area who make a living at lettering, and she refers people to that extensive list when asked.

She is a longtime member of the Society for Calligraphy, Southern California. She helps support the guild Website, with content and photo galleries. She has helped behind the scenes at many International Conferences.

C.C. has taken classes with Thomas Ingmire, Denis Brown, Judy Melvin, Michael Harvey and many, many other inspiring teachers. Her first calligraphy teacher, in 1987, was Elizabeth Lucas. She has a certificate in Calligraphy from the Extension program at California State University, Long Beach, where her teachers were Lucas, Lisa Engelbrecht, Barbara Close and Dick Pio. She also attended the program at Cerritos College (CA) with Marcia Brady.

Her "real job" is at Long Beach City College (CA), where she is an Educational Technologist / Multimedia Graphic Artist, where she supports faculty members in their efforts to integrate instructional technology into the curriculum. She assists colleagues with presentation design, web graphics, photo manipulation, charts and concept maps, photo composites, and much more. She has a master's degree in Educational Technology.

She enjoys reading and buying art supplies for her young nephews.

MARCY SCHNEIDER

82, 146

Artistic endeavors interested Marcy ever since she was a child. Thankfully her parents, who sent her to art classes, encouraged her. She became enamored with calligraphy accidentally when her mother suggested she take a class so she could address her twin brother's Bar Mitzvah invitations. The rest, as they say, is history.

Marcy is a member of Cream City Calligraphers of Milwaukee, Wisconsin, where she served for many years as workshop chair. This gave her the opportunity to work with numerous professional calligraphers and expand her experience even further. Under her tenure the guild hosted Dick Beasley, Leana Fay, Carol Pallesen, Barbara Close, Barry Morentz, Reggie Ezell, Carl Rohrs, Eliza Holliday, Nancy Culmone and Sheila Waters, just to name a few.

Marcy looks forward to the magic of conference each year and has attended nine past magical conferences.

MAUREEN SQUIRES

22, 128

As a student of Roman and other letterforms, Maureen enjoys taking the words of wonderful writers and poets and trying to express their meanings through the use of the appropriate alphabet in combination with color, illustration, illumination or abstract gesture. Writing whose appearance, as well as content, evokes response in the viewer. Maureen's background is Fine Arts and she was a painting major at Seton Hill University in western Pennsylvania. She first studied calligraphy as part of a Drawing and Design course. Several years after graduation she went back to Carnegie Mellon University and studied Advanced Calligraphy for two years with noted calligrapher, type-designer, Professor Arnold Bank, a turning point in her approach to the alphabet and painting. Her work since then has consisted primarily of "painting letters and words". Maureen enjoys interpreting the words of others or simply experimenting with the abstract forms of the alphabet in many historical and contemporary styles. Her tools range from traditional steel nibs, pointed and flat brushes to reeds, bamboo and as she puts it, "anything that writes". She writes with ink, liquid acrylic, gouache, Japanese watercolors and acrylic paint.
www.maureensquires.com

AMY VEANER

86

Ever since her mother told her " to go practice your handwriting", Amy Schupler Veaner has been doing just that. As a professional lettering artist her designs have been seen around the globe used in wedding invitations, personalized stationery, holiday cards, rubber stamps, greeting cards and more. A love of stitching and sewing sometimes finds its way into mixed media work. Most recently the discovery of printmaking and all its processes, has captivated her interest and creatively more doors continue to open. Amy holds a BFA in illustration from RISD and is married to Bo Veaner for 32 years. They have two sons Zach and Adam…and in naming them, have covered the alphabet, from Z to A.

GWEN WEAVER

Although I have been trained in the broad edged pen, I've fallen completely and desperately in love with the pointed pen. I attended a six week class at the Smithsonian Museum in Washington, DC in 1982 and the rest is history! I relocated in that same year from Maryland to Virginia Beach, Virginia and was fortunate to find the Tidewater Calligrapher's Guild. Although our guild folded years ago, we all benefitted enormously from classes and instructors that the Guild sponsored. I've had the pleasure of studying with many gifted instructors, both at Conferences and workshops.

I've been teaching my pointed pen personalities all across the US and Canada for many years starting in the mid 80's. I love traveling and meeting so many fascinating calligraphers and artists. I've taught at the Boston Conference in 2001, Legacies in 2005 and Letterforum in 2006 and Chicago 2008. I've been delighted to be a presenter at IAMPETH for many years including in New Orleans only a week before Katrina hit. I presented Romantically Roman in 2009 in Nashville in the company of some pretty amazing artists and will be in Orlando in 2010 presenting Thick and Thin. This wonderful group of Master Pen People is open to all of my "different" stuff – Weaver Writing, Romantically Roman, Copperplate, PenGwen, Thick and Thin and even Celtic Knots!

My work has been exhibited at many of the International Conferences and at other venues including The National Cathedral in Washington, DC, The Graceful Envelope, The Days of the Handmade Book, Alpha-Mark, Visual Voices, the Newberry Library, Strathmore Hall, the Donnell Library and others. I've been published in Letter Arts Reviews, Glen's Calendars, Bound and Lettered, Somerset Magazine, The Art and Craft of Hand Lettering, Scripsit and many other guild presentations.

Gwen Can be reached at:
5279 East Valleyside Court Virginia Beach, Virginia 23464
757-351-0195 home studio and fax or 757-373-1793 cell

SHARON ZEUGIN

Sharon Zeugin is a full time artist who lives with her family in Austin, Texas. A former social worker and therapist, Sharon studied calligraphy at the Roehampton Institute in London, and her interests include music, drawing, painting, history, mythology, literature, psychology, art, yoga, swimming and running. Art journals, multi-media drawings, paintings, collages and books are vehicles for Sharon's art, with themes ranging from personal reflections and political commentary, inner landscapes and dreams, and women's issues. In addition to classes offered privately and through the local art museum school, Sharon teaches all over the USA and Canada. Her award winning artwork is exhibited both locally and nationally, and has appeared in books and publications such as Letter Arts Review and the Art and Craft of Handlettering.

ALESIA ZORN

Calligrapher Alesia Zorn, a former Massachusettsite who dearly loves Fall in New England, now resides in Portland, Oregon, where she's become quite fond of rain. While most of her business is wedding work, she has been known to write on unusual things such as Native American drums, a peace pipe, walls & doors, glass, seashells & sand dollars and, once, even toast. You can find what projects she's been up to on her blog www.alesiazorn.typepad.com and her website www.alesiazorn.com.

We are grateful to each other for continuing with this project during some personally challenging times. This is our first publishing venture. It has been a somewhat daunting but extremely rewarding experience. So many people have helped us along the way and for that we are most grateful. A special THANK YOU to all of the calligraphers who have contributed their talent and time to this project. Without them, this book would not exist. We thank Milan for his photography tips and lending us his lights. Thanks to Mary and Meredith at Dynagraf who patiently helped these rookies learn the ropes. We want to thank all our family and friends who have encouraged us and offered all kinds of assistance with this labor of love. Also, we appreciate Cheryl's partner, Cathleen, and Cheryl's manager, Tony, for all their help and support. Finally, we whole-heartedly thank Cheryl Wheeler whose songs greatly enrich our lives. She is such a kind and generous person who did not hesitate to give her time to proofread lyrics, pose for pictures, as well as express her enthusiasm for the artwork. There is no one like Cheryl and we feel so lucky to be a part of such a unique project with her.

Cheryl Wheeler concerts are not to be missed. For more information about this talented singer-songwriter and to find her touring schedule, visit her website cherylwheeler.com

Her latest CD is Pointing At The Sun, released on her own label, Dias Records in 2009.